PRAISE FOR
LIFE UNDER THE CROSS

Dr. Johnston introduces a new generation to a hero of confessional Lutheranism: Matthias Flacius Illyricus. Like all our heroes, Flacius had his flaws, and Dr. Johnston's short biography does not gloss over them. Yet Flacius' courage in confessing the Gospel and his unique contributions to Lutheran scholarship in the sixteenth century are worthy of our admiration and appreciation. The suffering he endured, both because of his courageous confession and his stubbornness, made his life truly one lived under the cross. And the message of Christ's cross marked who he was and how he lived.

Rev. Prof. Joel Otto
professor of church history
Wisconsin Lutheran Seminary, Mequon, Wisconsin

In *Life Under the Cross*, Dr. Wade Johnston gives a fine description of the life and theological teaching of Matthias Flacius Illyricus. Although massively influential as a theologian, particularly in the theology of the Formula of Concord, Flacius has unfortunately been forgotten, misunderstood, and maligned because of his poorly worded and sadly misunderstood formulation of the doctrine of original sin. With wit and erudition, Dr. Johnston has provided a scholarly yet popular and easy-to-understand introduction to the life and legacy of Flacius. Lay students and scholars will both benefit from reading this short biography.

Jack Kilcrease
Lutheran lay theologian
professor of historical and systematic theology
Institute of Lutheran Theology, Brookings, South Dakota

LIFE UNDER THE CROSS

A BIOGRAPHY OF THE REFORMER MATTHIAS FLACIUS ILLYRICUS

WADE JOHNSTON

CONCORDIA PUBLISHING HOUSE · SAINT LOUIS

To my father, John Richard Johnston,
a Matthias on eighteen wheels, who instilled a love for history in me on walks he might not even remember and modeled a love for God and truth in ways I will never forget. He seldom puts words on paper, but when he does, he means them, and those are the only kinds of words that belong on a page.

Published by Concordia Publishing House
3558 S. Jefferson Ave., St. Louis, MO 63118-3968
1-800-325-3040 • cph.org

Manufactured in the United States of America

1 2 3 4 5 6 7 8 9 10 34 33 32 31 30 29 28 27 26 25

CONTENTS

FOREWORD

Most people forgotten by history deserve this collective amnesia. While their days and deeds influenced those closest to them, their circle of influence was too small to merit attention from subsequent generations. The rural parish pastors in Saxony during Martin Luther's lifetime, for instance, are a mere footnote in history. While they shaped the spiritual life of those in their villages in the sixteenth century, today they are remembered mostly for their theological ignorance that inspired Luther to write the catechisms.

Matthias Flacius Illyricus is an exception to this rule. Here is the rare forgotten historical figure who deserves more attention. His broad influence extended beyond his lifetime through his theological works, theological errors, and well-known irascibility. The generations of Lutheran pastors following Flacius benefited from his texts on hermeneutics (*Clavis Scripturae*), church history (*Magdeburg Centuries*), and other writings. And even now, when few know those works and far fewer read them, their indirect influence lives on because of the role each played in shaping hermeneutics and church history. Knowing more about this formative figure for Lutheran theology is just one reason to learn more about Flacius.

Flacius also serves as a model for Lutheran theology and practice, even as Flacius himself sought to emulate Luther. Yet Flacius, like few other people, is also a cautionary role model. With the exception of Christ Jesus, every person we identify as a role model was or is a sinful human being. As such, not everything they do sets a pattern for us to imitate. Sometimes the most powerful lessons we can draw from a model are what *not* to do. By all means, imitate the apostle Paul; but do not start your career by persecuting Christians. Yes, imitate Luther; but do not become so frustrated with a congregation that you quit preaching for the better part of a year.

Flacius provides virtuous acts and a disposition to emulate, as well as excesses and mistakes to avoid. His career offers a model of theological courage and integrity. He identified areas of need (hermeneutical insight, better-organized church history, clarity on the relationship of church and state, the definition of adiaphora, the right of resistance to authority, etc.) and skillfully met them. His refusal to compromise the Gospel of Jesus Christ in the face of political pressure is a model of courageous faithfulness to the truth. Yet his flaws are impossible to miss. His teaching concerning original sin is condemned by the same Formula of Concord that affirms his stance on adiaphora. And his stubbornness and pride caused him to stand by his understanding of original sin despite interventions by friends and colleagues to return him to the truth of Scripture. Place the good and the bad alongside each other, and Flacius stands as a caution that one not confuse a bold, unyielding confession of the truth with a prideful, stubborn refusal to be corrected when wrong.

A nuanced approach to theological role models is rare. It is far easier and more satisfying to count a theologian as either hero or villain, then affirm everything the hero does and condemn everything the villain does. Such a reductive approach appeals to our sinful heart and its pride, always eager to cast ourselves as unqualified, unflawed heroes. This reductive approach is also appealing because of the complexity of late-Reformation Lutheranism, with its dozens of theologians debating multiple issues through shifting alliances across several decades. Identifying heroes and villains requires serious and prolonged study, which makes it tempting to paint with broad brushstrokes. When we cannot remember the exact chronology of events or how the Adiaphoristic Controversy related to the Osiandrian Controversy, our prideful hearts take comfort in knowing, for example, that Philip Melanchthon was wrong concerning ceremonies. And clinging to that conclusion, we both congratulate ourselves for our wisdom and excuse ourselves for not knowing anything more about the question, the time period, or the context.

Wade Johnston avoids such simplistic readings and instead presents Flacius in such a way that the reader can see him as a flawed, sinful model of faithfully confessing Christ. Johnston does not shy away from this paradox. He highlights Flacius' brilliant moments and achievements without belittling, excusing, or overlooking his errors and misjudgments. Flacius shines through the pages as a thoroughly sinful human being who was a baptized child of God, knew his Savior, and aimed to do His will. Striving for truth and unity, Flacius nevertheless played a role in the fracturing of Lutheranism during his lifetime. For example, as Johnston demonstrates, Flacius succeeded in preserving the Gospel because he opposed the Leipzig Interim, but his extensive propaganda campaign made it an unforgivable sin to support the Interim. Without the possibility of forgiveness, the parties among the Lutherans were inevitably divided with little (no?) hope for reconciliation.

Insight into Flacius as a nuanced theological role model is but one reason to read this biography. Even as it focuses on Flacius, the book is an accessible entry into the complex world of late-Reformation Lutheranism. Johnston clearly presents the subtle and complex questions that characterize this period. His theological insight offers distinctions that reveal the opposing views and the stakes in the controversies swirling around Flacius.[1] Having read this book, the reader can read or revisit the Formula of Concord with an increased understanding of the controversies addressed there. As both a historian and a theologian, Johnston skillfully recounts the story of Flacius' life and work, demonstrating how God works through sinful human beings in the history of the church.

Johnston also gives an admirable example of charity extended to flawed human actors. Punctuated here and there with good humor, and situated within adequate historical context to understand why charity ought to be extended, Johnston is gracious in his account while still condemning errors. In addition to a better understanding of Flacius, Johnston notes his own increased understanding of Melanchthon and his actions, even when he made the wrong choices.

---

1 For more comprehensive exploration of this period, see Friedrich Bente, *Historical Introductions to the Lutheran Confessions*, 2nd ed. (St. Louis: Concordia Publishing House, 2005); Robert Kolb and James A. Nestingen, *Sources and Contexts of the Book of Concord* (Minneapolis: Fortress Press, 2001); Charles P. Arand, James A. Nestingen, and Robert Kolb, *The Lutheran Confessions: History and Theology of the Book of Concord* (Minneapolis: Fortress Press, 2012).

Such charity shows a deeper wisdom than that of the actors in this historical drama, whom Johnston identifies as "too indomitable and smart for their own good" as they turn on one another and refuse to be corrected.[2]

Johnston's efforts have resulted in this introduction to one of the most influential Lutheran theologians, a man who deserves more than the scant attention he receives. The work highlights the grace of God in preserving His church through the work of sinful human beings. It is a reminder that we are yet another generation of sinful human beings redeemed by Christ. Let us seek to uphold the truth without falling into prideful traps and self-righteousness that confuses stubborn adherence to clumsy formulations with faithful confession of the truth of God's Word; that mistakes petty quarreling for refutation of error; that frames refusal of forgiveness as faithfulness to Christ. Read. Mark. Avoid the arrogance, pride, and stubbornness of Flacius. Imitate the good by faithfully confessing Christ and striving to uphold the truth of the Gospel with courage, but do so with more grace than Flacius could muster.

You will find in these pages, I suspect, insights that go beyond Flacius, such as Johnston's argument that "Flacius' confession was who he was, not just what he believed."[3] I think Johnston is right, and I am left asking if this approach to confessing the faith is helpful, detrimental, or both. Does it arm one properly for the faithful confession of the truth, even in the face of persecution, mockery, or belittlement? Does it set one up to defend errors that, as part of one's identity, are nearly impossible to abandon? Does it put my confession in the place of Christ as the way, the truth, and the life; that is, should I build my identity on my confession of Christ or on Christ Himself? Even as Matthew 16 runs through my mind, I do not have answers for you. But as you read this book, consider how that dynamic led Flacius both to heroic acts and to grievous errors.

Aaron Moldenhauer
Vice President for Mission and Church Relations
Concordia University Wisconsin and Ann Arbor
All Saints' Day 2024

2 See below, p. 64.

3 See below, p. 28.

LIFE UNDER THE CROSS

INTRODUCTION

Matthias Flacius Illyricus is one of the most significant and polarizing figures in Protestant history. There is no way around him. Exegetes, historians, and systematic theologians have been shaped by him, whether they realize it or not. Protestant conceptions of the relationship between church and state, including our own in the United States, have been influenced by Flacius and his comrades and supporters. The fields of hermeneutics and church history—whether Protestant or Roman Catholic—have him as a father. He is one of the single most productive and profound theologians Germany has ever produced, and he was a Croatian. He is perhaps one of the most important scholars that scholars simply do not write about.

I have been interested in Matthias Flacius Illyricus since I first heard about him. He has that effect on people. It is hard to meet Flacius and not think something—it seems you either want to know more or think you know too much already. He is perhaps only slightly less controversial today than he was during his lifetime. He is hard to ignore, as much as some might wish he were not. For those who trace their theological roots to Martin Luther, it is almost impossible to make sense of Lutheranism without knowledge of Flacius. In many ways, he represents the best of Luther and Melanchthon, even as he remained a dogged defender of the former to his own detriment and became a thorn in the side of the latter.

There are few things today that we could call Flacius that he was not called in his lifetime. Brilliant, stubborn, untiring, tiring, perceptive, dismissive, faithful, ungrateful, divisive, charismatic—the Croatian has been called it all. He helped Luther's teachings survive the threats of the sixteenth century and yet also thwarted attempts at unity within Lutheranism. He carefully dissected the doctrinal formulations of others and yet, when caught, refused to retract incautious language of his own. He established complex networks throughout Europe and yet lost one friend after another throughout his career. Even more telling, in some corners of Lutheranism he is blamed for having a spirit anathema to churchmanship while in others he has been celebrated as a tenacious and self-sacrificing defender of orthodoxy worthy of emulation. Depending on whom you ask, Protestantism has had way too many Flacii[1] or is in desperate need of more.

Historians and theologians alike feel compelled to diagnose Flacius when they write about him. I claim no immunity. Nevertheless, scholarship about the man has suffered because of this. Seldom has his work been considered apart from his personality. He was an innovator in more than a handful of fields, and a father in several, and yet the historiography bears out the truism that scandal sells. Although much of his work was not polemical, his publications are consistently read as those of a controversialist. Counterfactual history is the stuff of historical fiction, and yet one wonders what Flacius would have been had he lived in different times and circumstances.

The benefit of this historiographical reality, however, is that what has been written about Flacius has often betrayed as much about the author as the subject. Again, I claim no immunity. I am not an impartial observer. I come at Flacius as a product of my age and as someone with clear theological and cultural convictions. I have tried to mitigate this fact, but evidence of it surely abounds in this work. The same is true of readers. For many of us, Flacius is bound to be a hero or villain before we give him a meaningful hearing. The same is true of Melanchthon, his teacher, and of Flacius' various opponents. We might as well be honest about that. And maybe, in recognizing as much, we can do more justice to all involved in the controversies after Luther's death. Studying Flacius has made me more sympathetic, not less, toward his opponents, especially the great *Praeceptor*

1 Or Flaciuses?

Germaniae, Flacius' teacher and mentor, Philip Melanchthon. I have grown in my appreciation for the great Wittenberger's teaching and for what led to his actions in the tumultuous years of the interims. I still like to think that I would have done differently as a Lutheran pastor, but I no longer consider his actions quite so unfathomable. The same is true of other Wittenbergers. These are men all Lutherans celebrate until 1546. In Luther biographies, they are heroes, willing to risk their lives to support Martin, the prophet and herald. They were that, to some degree. But they were human, both during Luther's life and after. While there were shifts and breaks that happened in the controversies after Luther's death, we should never forget that every person is a warehouse of shifts and breaks. These were the same men throughout, and there was never a time when they were not. Their differences were not the stuff of Marvel movies, of heroes and villains, so much as products of their times and circumstances. Most were trying to do the best they could with the hand they were dealt. They deserve that consideration in hindsight. We do no favors for them or ourselves with anachronism or chronological hubris. This is true of Flacius as well. Please bear with me, then, as I try to afford him that charity in what follows, and as I betray my own person, story, and convictions as I do so.

This biography is not meant to be the final say on anything. It is not intended to be authoritative. Those biographies have been written or will be written by others. Wilhelm Preger's two-volume biography of Flacius in German is still the gold standard.[2] Oliver Olson sparked a Flacius revival in English with the first volume of his biography.[3] I eagerly await the second volume and thank him for the amazing amount of scholarship he has brought to print about Flacius. He has also been extremely kind to me, encouraging me when I undertook my graduate work with the intention of writing on Flacius and sharing insights and resources with me. In addition to Olson's biography, there is another outstanding Flacius biography in English. Luka Ilić has done the church and historians in general an enormous favor with his work. His biography is outstanding, and the number of publications

---

2 Wilhelm Preger, *Matthias Flacius Illyricus und seine Zeit,* 2 vols. (Erlangen: T. Bläsing, 1859–61).

3 Oliver K. Olson, *Matthias Flacius and the Survival of Luther's Reform* (Wiesbaden: Harrassowitz, 2002).

he has produced in addition to it is extremely impressive.[4] The conferences he has organized and his promotion of Flacius studies have left a lasting mark upon the field. On more than one occasion I have wondered when he finds time to sleep.

So why this biography? There are several reasons, none of them profound. First, I have wanted to write it for years for my own good. I have written and presented on various aspects of Flacius' work and stages of his life and found that very rewarding, but I have wanted to spend time working slowly through his time and labors on this earth from start to finish. Second, I am convinced that Matthias Flacius Illyricus should be a name more familiar in Lutheranism, Protestantism, and the Christian Church in general. Like him or hate him, agree with his teachings or reject them, knowing this man and his thought gives one a better understanding of a crucial part of the history of Christianity, its thought and practices, the Scriptures and their interpretation, the church's conceptions of its history across time, and the significance of understanding those conceptions. Precisely because he was an outsider at home—an Evangelical living under the threat of the Venetian Inquisition—and then in Germany as a contentious figure in a fractured Protestantism, Flacius gives us insight into more than himself. Third, while there are great resources available, I think there is a need for one that is affordable, accessible, and knows when to say amen for those dipping their toes into the topic. The parish pastor in me is captive to the belief that there is not much use doing something pertaining to the church unless the average layperson or pastor will find that it is beneficial, that they can afford to care about it, and that they will have opportunity, in a feasible and practical way, to build on their time spent with what I have written. I hope some of my footnotes point readers to valuable new reads too.

I am a trained theologian and historian. I have served in pastoral ministry in the parish and as a professor in academia. My doctorate is in history. As I have approached this work, I have asked myself if I am doing history or theology, or historical theology. I like to think that I have functioned primarily as a historian, but I think that is

4 Luka Ilić, *Theologian of Sin and Grace: The Process of Radicalization in the Theology of Matthias Flacius Illyricus* (Göttingen: Vandenhoeck & Ruprecht, 2014).

wishful thinking in a number of ways and places. If I am honest, my own theology, the theology of my church body, and the theology of the greater fellowship to which my church body used to belong, the Synodical Conference, has been profoundly influenced by Flacius. I have sought to do history here while being sympathetic without being partisan. I do think I have largely succeeded in that. That being said, I know I have blind spots. I would like to be honest about some of those from the past of which I have become aware, so let me say a little about Friedrich Bente, his *Historical Introductions to the Lutheran Confessions* (which was included in the *Concordia Triglotta* edition of the Book of Concord),[5] and my corner of American Lutheranism.

Bente's introduction to the Book of Concord is a valuable resource. There are few like it. It fills many voids. Without it, many Lutheran pastors might go into the parish with a big gap in their knowledge of the time between Luther's death and the Formula of Concord. Moreover, they may not appreciate everything that went into figuring out what it was to be a Lutheran without Luther. It is critical for Lutherans to understand that there were no glory years. There never was some Evangelical utopia. From its beginning, Protestantism had a tenuous hold on the Gospel. Luther knew this. He warned about it often. Bente has done Lutheran churches a favor by driving home all that went into preserving Gospel preaching in Germany.

So what is the issue, then? Why do I bring it up? The problem (and this problem is more the reader's fault than the author's perhaps) is that Bente's work sometimes seems too much like a classic Western movie. The good guys and bad guys are obvious. This lends itself to partisan history. Readers form easy caricatures and later call to mind simplified narratives. Heroes are celebrated and villains vilified. It is forgotten that many of these "villains" spent much of their life under a very real threat of martyrdom. A sort of confessionalism emerges that is not always healthy, biblical, or historical. It becomes an aesthetic.

I do not necessarily blame Bente for this. It is no accident that I have mentioned him though (a Flacius joke, just to lighten the mood). Seminarians are in a formative stage of life—intentionally so. They soak in ideas and consider the parish and pastoral ministry largely in the abstract. There are all sorts of things they are going to do when they get out, exciting things, and these things are shaped

5 For a reprint of only *Historical Introductions*, see above, p. ix n. 1.

by their studies and those whom they study. And as they study the heroes and villains of church history, seminarians create a spectrum and hope to fall somewhere on it. I hope most want not to be villains. I am sure I have been one at times.

Bente's depiction of Flacius led many seminarians to celebrate his tenacious spirit. Sure, he made some mistakes, but he was a true warrior for sound doctrine and proper practice. He fought the right fights, even if he had some missteps in the midst of them. Celebrating this Flacian spirit, this caricature of a complex man, is not unlike the improper use of Luther's "sin boldly" counsel as an excuse to behave like a donkey. It does not facilitate faithful ministry; it undermines it. It is not unlike the seminarians who would celebrate smoking a cigar or enjoying a whiskey to prove they were not pietists. They were not actually undermining pietism through such indulgence. They merely became pietists having a cigar or a whiskey. One could argue they became more dangerous pietists than the pietists they were resolute not to be. Historian though I have striven to be in this undertaking, I have been that Flacian. I have been that pietist. And so this is my confession. I have repented of it. I have worked on it. I have learned to actually enjoy a cigar or whiskey instead of sacralizing it as an instrument of self-justification and a righteousness of my own invention. But that fake little Flacius is still in there somewhere, and if he has come out on these pages and exposed himself for the fool that he is, I apologize to the reader in advance, and to Matthias.

LUTHER AND FLACIUS

A DEEP DEPRESSION HAD overtaken Matthias Flacius Illyricus in Wittenberg. He missed his family, even those unhappy with his journey north. This new climate was very different, and not in a pleasant way. The food also did not please him. And yet Flacius saw his depression first and foremost as a theological crisis.

> At the end of my third year living in Wittenberg, when I was staying in the home of Dr. Friedrich Backofen . . . and the torment had become so desperate that I thought I was going to die soon, he saw that I could no longer study on account of this tribulation, and he prevailed upon me to tell him why. After he had questioned me, he comforted me and prayed for me and worked it out through Dr. Pomeranus[1] for me to see Dr. Martin Luther.[2]

In Luther, Flacius found someone who knew such struggles well. Luther shared his own experience and that of others. He spoke the

1 I.e., Johann Bugenhagen.

2 Matthias Flacius Illyricus, *Entschuldigung Matthiae Flacij Illyrici, geschrieben an die Universitet zu Wittemberg der Mittelding halben. Item sein brief an Philip. Melanthonem sampt etlichen andern schrifften dieselbige sach belangend. Verdeudscht* (Magdeburg: Christian Rödinger, 1549), Er.

Word of God for consolation. Prayers were said in the church for Flacius. His condition slowly improved "day by day" until he recovered. Flacius "had not revealed the matter [of his suffering] to anyone" for three years, but now, having confessed to Backofen and spoken with Luther, he found hope.[3]

This experience marked Flacius' life and person. He connected this incident to his certainty of his calling as a teacher of God's Word and defender of the same.[4] Luther's Reformation was not an intellectual interest for him, he insisted. He was not looking for abstractions. He had experienced Law and Gospel. It had been done to him. He had gone through the same struggles as Luther. He, like Luther, had his life changed dramatically by and for the Good News of Jesus Christ. That was the reason he was in Wittenberg to begin with, and it was in Wittenberg that Luther had personally done for Flacius what Luther's message did for so many: freed him from despair. Flacius knew *tentatio*, or *Anfechtung* (that is, testing), well. As was said later of Paul Gerhardt, the great Lutheran hymn writer, Flacius had been sifted in the devil's sieve. Christ had delivered him. This conviction drove all the sacrifice, scholarship, and stubbornness that Flacius would endure, produce, and exhibit in the bitter years to come. For all that came before and after, this is what made Flacius who he was. He had learned the Gospel, not merely from academic study but also through lived experience, as "Dr. Luther would have a theologian learn it" and as "the Scriptures also commend in Christ," and nothing was going to take that Gospel from Flacius, or anyone else, without a fight.[5]

Early Life and Education

Matthias Flacius (Matija Vlačić) was born March 3, 1520, the year of Luther's famous "three treatises."[6] Named after the disciple chosen to

3 Flacius Illyricus, *Entschuldigung Matthiae Flacij Illyrici*, Er.

4 Preger, *Matthias Flacius Illyricus*, 1:23.

5 Flacius Illyricus, *Entschuldigung Matthiae Flacij Illyrici*, Ev.

6 I.e., *To the Christian Nobility of the German Nation*, AE 44:115–217; *The Babylonian Captivity of the Church*, AE 36:3–126; *The Freedom of a Christian*, AE 31:327–77.

replace Judas as an apostle, his name, Matthias, means "gift of God."[7] His birthplace was Albona (modern-day Labin), a small city with a little more than a thousand people. Albona was located on the Istrian Peninsula, stretching down into the Adriatic Sea, part of what had been the ancient Roman province of Illyria. As a result, "Illyricus" often followed "Flacius" as part of the name by which the great theologian would be known. Matthias' birthplace also perhaps helps to explain his gift for languages, as Croatian was the language of the home and Italian that of culture and government.

His father was Andreas Vlačić, also called Frankowitz (Frankovich). After centuries of speculation about the origin of the Frankowitz name, nothing certain is known. While the family's origins were plebian, the Vlačićs were at the time of Matthias' birth a patrician family in Albona, established over three generations, and his father was a relatively well-to-do man. A small landowner, Andreas Vlačić appears to have been an enthusiastic scholar in his own right.

Matthias' mother, Jacobea Luciani, was of more noteworthy lineage than her husband, as was the case for Luther's parents. Her family was prominent in Albona and had been for quite some time, unlike the Vlačićs. Together with the Lupetinos, the Lucianis and the Vlačićs guided the civic life of Albona at the time of Matthias' birth. Sadly, it appears that Jacobea died in childbirth. After Andreas' death, Matthias' uncle Luciano Luciani, a judge and longtime supporter of Venetian rule, was appointed his guardian. The Lupetino family would also play an important role in the boy's life and development. Baldo Lupetino, Luciano's brother-in-law, would help precipitate Matthias' later move north to Germany.

Beginning at an early age, Matthias' education was a priority. He first studied with his father and later with Franciscus Ascerius of Milan. Matthias was a gifted student; his schooling eventually took him to Venice (at this time, Albona was under Venetian control), where he studied under Giovanni Battista Egnazio. In Venice, Matthias received a solid humanist training in keeping with the times. He was steeped in the classics and developed a lifelong love for ancient manuscripts. He paid attention to the civic life of the city and

7 The Feast of St. Matthias was celebrated on February 24 in the Middle Ages. It was decided during Vatican II to move the observance to May 14 so that it would not fall during Lent.

attended meetings pertaining to it. As so many aspiring humanists had done before him, including Melanchthon and Luther, he adapted his name, latinizing it. He became "Flacius" and would be known as such for the rest of his life: Matthias Flacius Illyricus. Later in life, as Ilić notes, he would begin adding another geographic reference to his name, perhaps longing for the land of his childhood after decades of controversies, crosses, and nomadic life: "Albonensis," recalling his beautiful hometown on the Adriatic Sea.[8]

Matthias Flacius was sixteen when he set off for Venice, a city where the Renaissance had long ago taken root, home to the publishing house of Aldus Manutius and the bright minds and creative spirits it attracted. Flacius' education there prepared him for the towering interdisciplinary intellectual life to come. He studied at San Marco, the progressive school in Venice, and was heavily influenced by its hunger for ancient texts, languages, and learning. Here Flacius studied and edited classical manuscripts, honing the skills that would define his later work in bookselling and historical and theological scholarship: finding, analyzing, authenticating, cataloging, publishing texts, or summarizing their contents in publications, or procuring them for others. He became acquainted with wide swaths of historical, religious, and cultural literature from antiquity through the medieval period, a knowledge he later put to good use in illustrations and as evidence for his arguments against the papacy and in support for Luther's teaching.

Surprisingly, Flacius did not write much about his teacher in Venice, Egnazio, a longtime associate of Manutius and an acquaintance of many leading humanists, including Desiderius Erasmus of Rotterdam and Melanchthon, exchanging letters with both. Olson speculates that this may be because Egnazio was sympathetic to Lutheranism and thus at risk of persecution by the Inquisition.[9] This makes sense. Producing the most notorious Croatian Lutheran of all time, and one of the most notorious anywhere in Europe in the sixteenth century, likely would raise some suspicions.

Flacius later reported that while he was still in Venice he became suspicious of some of the piety and practice he witnessed in the

8 Ilić, *Theologian of Sin and Grace*, 33.

9 Olson, *Matthias Flacius and the Survival of Luther's Reform*, 31.

churches. It seems his reading of the Scriptures had produced a questioning spirit and left its mark.[10] By all accounts, however, he was still a faithful son of the Roman Church, increasingly desirous of becoming a theologian within her ranks, even if it meant becoming a monk.[11] This led him to Baldo Lupetino, his uncle's brother-in-law, a learned Franciscan monk and gifted preacher. Flacius would later call him his "preceptor of truth."[12] At the time, Flacius wanted help becoming a lay brother so he could study theology further.

Baldo Lupetino was a secret devotee of Luther's theology. He introduced Flacius to Luther's writings and encouraged him to study in Germany, where he could better learn Evangelical theology. At nineteen, having finished his studies, Flacius took Lupetino's advice and escaped the Inquisition, which was picking up its pace in Venice after a period of surprising laxity regarding the dissemination of Luther's writings. Not long after Flacius' departure in 1539, the budding Lutheran circles in Venice were all but wiped out.[13] Because of Lupetino's advice, Flacius survived, leaving everything he had ever known and the future he had been building, against his family's wishes and without their financial support, to head for the lands of the reformations. From Germany, Flacius would do more than almost any German to preserve and promulgate Luther's Gospel message.

The Road to Wittenberg

Flacius made his way to Augsburg, the city where the Evangelical princes and leaders had made their bold confession in 1530, what some have called the birth of the Evangelical Lutheran Church. Ilić explains that regular trade between Venice and Augsburg and frequent

10 Flacius Illyricus, *Entschuldigung Matthiae Flacij Illyrici*, Diiiiv.

11 Preger, *Matthias Flacius Illyricus und seine Zeit*, 1:14. Interestingly, Preger sees Flacius' later recollections as evidence of his peace of mind in Roman Catholicism, while Olson takes them as evidence of Evangelical inclinations before reading Luther (Olson, *Matthias Flacius and the Survival of Luther's Reform*, 28–29).

12 Preger, *Matthias Flacius Illyricus und seine Zeit*, 1:34.

13 Baldo Lupetino spent nearly fifteen years in captivity at the hands of the Venetian Inquisition and eventually was sentenced to death by drowning.

caravans back and forth likely determined Augsburg as Flacius' destination.[14] Arriving in Augsburg, he met the ecclesiastical superintendent, Bonifacius Wolfhardt (Lycosthenes), a Zwinglian. Wolfhardt recommended that Flacius continue on to Basel, home of a university and an established printing industry.[15] We do not know how long Flacius stayed in Augsburg, but he did make some important friends who would prove valuable later in life, corresponding with him and supporting publishing projects.[16] Flacius was a man who knew how to network, and he made the most of his time in Augsburg, however brief, as he so often did elsewhere.

Upon his move to Basel, Flacius became familiar with the reformation of Ulrich Zwingli and Johann Oecolampadius, which lived on after the reformers themselves had died and which still influenced Basel greatly. Wolfhardt also surely knew that in Basel Flacius could encounter more than reformation ideas. Basel had also been home to the great humanist Erasmus of Rotterdam. The Croatian would find in Basel a rich humanist intellectual culture to explore and enjoy, as he had in Venice.

Flacius enrolled at the University of Basel as "Matheus de Fanciscis of Albona of the diocese of Pola in Illyria, under Venetian rule, pauper."[17] That he was listed as a pauper meant that he was not obligated to pay full tuition. He befriended his professor Johannes Oporinus, who lectured on Greek and Hebrew and would later become a full-time printer, publishing a number of Flacius' works. Perhaps Oporinus increased Flacius' interest in Hebrew, for later Flacius would serve as a Hebrew professor on the faculty at the University of Wittenberg.

---

14 Ilić, *Theologian of Sin and Grace*, 41.

15 Matthias Flacius Illyricus, "Erzehlunge der Handlungen oder Religionsstreiten und Sachen Matthiae Fl. Jllyrici von jm selbs trewlich und warhafftiglich auff Beger der Prediger zu Strasburg beschrieben Anno 1568," in Caspar Heldelin, *Eine Christliche predigt uber der Leiche des Ehrnwüdigen und hochgelerten Herrn M: Matthiae Flacij Illyrici Weiland getrewen Dieners vnd bestendigen Merterers Jesu Christi Fromen Hertzen zu gut gestellet Durch M Casparum Heldelinum Lindauiensem Item Summarischer Bericht der Handlungen vnd Streitsachen Herrn Matthiae Flacij Illyrici von im selbst verzeichnet* (Oberursel: Nikolaus Henricus, 1575), Tiiv.

16 Ilić deserves credit for unpacking these contacts in a way that previous biographers have not: *Theologian of Sin and Grace*, 40ff.

17 Olson, *Matthias Flacius and the Survival of Luther's Reform*, 35.

Unlike many from the network Flacius established throughout his lifetime, Oporinus seems to have remained an unwavering friend to his former student until his death.

In Basel, Flacius lived in the house of Simon Grynaeus, a German theologian, recently appointed a professor at the university. Grynaeus was an accomplished humanist, a close friend and successor of Erasmus at Basel, and a talented theologian. In good humanist fashion, he took the name "Grynaeus" from Virgil. A fellow student of Melanchthon's at the Latin school in Pforzheim, Grynaeus had a gift for languages. He played a role in the Reformation in Württemberg and in the crafting of the First Helvetic Confession, which sought to unify Protestants. Fellow participants in the formation of that confession included reformers of such renown as Heinrich Bullinger and Leo Jud, Oswald Myconius, Martin Bucer, and Wolfgang Capito. Grynaeus lectured on Romans in Basel to great acclaim. Like Wolfhardt in Augsburg, he was a supporter of the Wittenberg Concord, which sought Lutheran-Reformed rapprochement on the Lord's Supper. In short, the "pauper" from Albona found himself in a prominent home. Flacius enjoyed his time in the household as well. He later recalled: "I lived with the very learned Simon Grynaeus . . . who received me at his table and treated me as if I were nothing other than his own biological son."[18] This is no small praise for him to give Grynaeus in 1568, after decades of theological strife, considering that Grynaeus' moderating views and ecumenical spirit stood at odds with Flacius' controversialist tact in the heated conflicts that arose following Luther's death.

Flacius' time in Basel was short but, as has been seen, formative. In addition to studying Greek and Hebrew, he also grew in his knowledge of philosophy.[19] He expanded his network. He learned how to navigate influential northern Reformation and humanist circles. He developed a better sense for the reforming movements beyond Germany. He adapted to a new climate and languages.

From Basel, Flacius moved on to the University of Tübingen, an institution Grynaeus had played an earlier role in reshaping. In Tübingen, Flacius lived and studied with another Croat, Matthias Garbitius Illyricus (Matija Grbić). Born in Istria, Garbitius also had

---

18 Flacius Illyricus, "Erzehlunge der Handlungen oder Religionsstreiten und Sachen," Tiiv.

19 Olson, *Matthias Flacius and the Survival of Luther's Reform*, 36.

moved north as a "pauper," as Flacius had been registered at the University of Basel. Garbitius studied at Heidelberg and then at Wittenberg with Luther and Melanchthon and had been a guest at the houses of both men on more than one occasion. Melanchthon thought very highly of Garbitius and commended him to others a number of times. It was Melanchthon's recommendation, in fact, that helped Garbitius obtain a professorship at Wittenberg, where he taught Greek literature. In 1537, he moved to Tübingen. Flacius appreciated the opportunity to stay with a countryman, and one who was so accomplished.

Garbitius and Joachim Camerarius the Elder[20] both encouraged and aided Flacius' later move to Wittenberg, where he, as Garbitius and Camerarius had earlier, became a student of Melanchthon. Flacius' very public disagreements with their former teacher soured the relationship with Camerarius, who scorned Flacius for his criticism of Melanchthon. Camerarius would not be the only friend Flacius would lose because of theological controversy.

In Tübingen, spiritual anguish, which he kept to himself, troubled Flacius. This likely had begun already in Basel and would continue in Wittenberg. Following a stop in Regensburg, where a religious colloquy was being held, Flacius made his way to Wittenberg. Surely he felt as if his long journey was at its end, bringing him to the feet of Luther and Melanchthon and the other gifted, steadfast reforming theologians in the city synonymous with Protestantism. Here he could find humanism and theology wedded in a dogged pursuit of biblical truth, the Gospel proclaimed in all its fullness, with clarity, and, surely he prayed, peace for his soul. If he was hoping to find in Wittenberg a bustling imperial free city like Augsburg, a dynamic cultural center like Venice, breathtaking natural beauty as in Albona, or an eclectic mix of theological perspectives as existed in Basel, he was disappointed. It is hard to believe any disappointment would have lasted long, however, because in Wittenberg he did find what he had been seeking most. His discoveries would drive everything he did, often at great personal risk and expense, for the rest of his life.

20 Camerarius would become Melanchthon's first biographer.

The Wittenberg Years

Matthias Flacius arrived in Wittenberg in 1541, enrolling as a student at the university on May 1. He had finally made his way home, he hoped, at least theologically. Having taken Baldo Lupetino's advice, he had now arrived at the source, the home of the theology that had moved Lupetino to show Matthias some of his secret stash of books and would move Lupetino to give his life rather than recant at the hands of the Venetian Inquisition. Flacius was a stranger in a strange land, but the Gospel had called him here, and he arrived in need of it, weary and tormented still by spiritual anguish. Ilić describes Flacius' early life in Wittenberg as consisting of "his room, the University and the church," so that he developed a reputation "for his utter devotion to research and serious scholarship."[21] Even in spiritual affliction, he wanted to make the most of the opportunity afforded him in Wittenberg after so much sacrifice, travel, and prayer.

Flacius' journey to Wittenberg exposed him to a variety of Protestant theology. He had established a diverse network. He continued to read widely at Wittenberg, including works by Bullinger, Bucer, and Erasmus. He was still a work in progress. While later his mind would latch on to what he considered the central truths of Luther's preaching and teaching, to hold them tight and preserve and proclaim them to others, he was still very open to ideas at this point. And as always, he made a number of friends, expanding his network.

The most important friend Flacius made in Wittenberg was Philip Melanchthon. Flacius lodged in the home of this prominent theologian, in a prominent location in Wittenberg, right on the main street. Melanchthon found students for Flacius to instruct in Greek and Hebrew. Years later, both men spoke of how sincere and close their friendship had been during these years before Luther's death. Surely both were hurt because of the position the other had taken when doctrinal controversy arose. The disappointment and resentment of later years, however, ought not diminish the fondness that sprouted between these two great minds and the intimate working relationship they developed.

---

21 Ilić, *Theologian of Sin and Grace*, 62.

His spiritual struggles finally over, thanks to Luther's consolation and the teaching of justification by faith alone, Flacius was able to commit himself to his studies with renewed vigor. His goal—an ambitious one—was to become a professor in Wittenberg. As a result of demonstrating his gifts in his interactions with the faculty and through his research and scholarship, he was appointed a professor of Hebrew in 1544 at the age of twenty-four, no small feat, especially for one who had come from so far away. Olson relates that Flacius was chosen for the position as a result of his popularity with students, who would converge on him outside class time to ask questions about Hebrew or Greek.[22] This popularity led Chancellor Gregor Brück to recommend Flacius to the elector. Along with Melanchthon's high praise, this proved decisive in his appointment to the faculty. The new Hebrew professor lectured on more than that language. He lectured on the Psalms; Paul's letters to the Romans, Corinthians, Ephesians, and Galatians; and Aristotle. Flacius completed his master's degree in February 1546, a week after Luther's death, ranking first in his class. His thesis argued that vowel pointing was original to the Hebrew text of the Old Testament. He took this stance against a rabbi who had lived in Venice during his time there. Flacius sought to defend the verbal inspiration of the Scriptures and argue against the church or anyone else standing in authority over the text. While Flacius turned out to be wrong,[23] the thesis shows Flacius' commitment to Reformation thought. During this period of his life in Wittenberg, Flacius also accumulated an impressive number of nicknames. Olson argues that many of them were likely a sign of affection rather than mockery.[24]

Interestingly, in a 1551 polemical text, while recalling his academic training in Wittenberg, Flacius emphasized that he was a student of Melanchthon and Luther, while making note of the fact that he did not attend any lectures by Johann Bugenhagen or Georg Major during this time.[25] When Flacius wrote this reflection, both Bugenhagen and

---

22 Olson, *Matthias Flacius and the Survival of Luther's Reform*, 52.

23 The pointing of the Hebrew text was added by a group of Jewish scribes (the Masoretes) sometime during the seventh to tenth centuries after Christ's birth.

24 Olson, *Matthias Flacius and the Survival of Luther's Reform*, 42.

25 Matthias Flacius Illyricus, *Gründliche verlegung aller Sophisterey, so D. Pfeffinger mit den andern Adiaphoristen, das Leiptzigsche Jnterim zubeschönen, gebraucht* (Magdeburg: Christian Rödinger, 1551), Hiiir.

Major had become "Adiaphorists" and "Interimists," as Flacius termed them, but so had Melanchthon. Moreover, Bugenhagen had been the one to bring Flacius to Luther during his spiritual anguish. It is surprising, therefore, that he would include Bugenhagen with Major as instructors he avoided, while presenting Melanchthon prominently as his teacher. This is a sign, no doubt, of how difficult it was for him to bear the conflict with his mentor, and this reticence to attack directly his former preceptor is evident in many of his writings. There is little reason to doubt his report, however. Flacius was a student of Luther and Melanchthon—and especially Melanchthon.[26] They, more than any others, made Flacius who he was in his own personal assessment. Like Luther, he was a student of the Old Testament. Like Melanchthon, he put his sharp, organized mind to work, carefully unpacking and presenting those things to which he gave his attention. Luther was the prophet; Melanchthon, the professor.

Flacius' arrival in Wittenberg actually brought him an opportunity to head home, or nearly so. In 1542, Baldo Lupetino had been imprisoned by the Venetian Inquisition for his preaching, which was winning converts for Reformation doctrines. The next year, Flacius set out for Venice with a letter from the leaders of the Schmalkaldic League, urging that Lupetino be released. He also brought a letter from Luther for the Evangelical community in Venice.[27] Flacius eventually found Lupetino in prison, surely a dreadful sight. This was Flacius' first personal experience with the Inquisition, having moved north before the major crackdown on Evangelicals in areas under Venetian control. Lupetino's words and his willingness to face martyrdom stuck with his fellow Istrian for life: "Non ricantare, anzi cantare! [Don't recant, rather sing!]." In this way, Lupetino formed and sent out Flacius to become the Slavic theologian of the German Reformation who would rival any native son in learning, courage, and zeal, with a cultural, political, and religious footprint discernible still today.[28]

26 For more on Flacius' relationship with the two great Wittenberg reformers, see Irene Dingel, "Flacius als Schüler Luthers und Melanchthons," in *Vestigia pietatis: Studien zur Geschichte der Frömmigkeit in Thüringen und Sachsen* (Leipzig: Evangelische Verlagsanstalt, 2000), 77–93.

27 Olson, *Matthias Flacius and the Survival of Luther's Reform*, 51.

28 Mijo Mirković, *Matija Vlačić Ilirik* (Zagreb: Jugoslavenska akademija znanosti i umietnosi, 1960), 489–90.

Flacius was the student of Luther and Melanchthon, but he was their student because of his mentor and countryman now in chains for the Gospel.[29] These three men, Luther, Melanchthon, and Lupetino, had captured Flacius' mind and heart. Surely the memory of Lupetino, so resolute in the direst of straits, played a role in Flacius' willingness to oppose his teacher and friend in the later controversies, albeit with great anguish, when Melanchthon urged a course around persecution rather than through it. Flacius drew on Lupetino's spirit to defend Melanchthon's teaching against Melanchthon, at least as he saw it.

Flacius married in November 1545, a development made possible by his professorship. His new wife, Elizabeth Faustus, was the daughter of a pastor. They would have twelve children during their marriage of twenty years, which ended with her death in 1564. The couple's courtship having been arranged at least in part by Melanchthon and the wedding attended by Luther, it was a thoroughly Wittenberg affair, one that surely delighted Flacius and made him proud. Preger calls this time the high point of his good fortune, the most joyous occasion of his time in Wittenberg and at any time to come.[30]

A close friendship and working relationship grew between Flacius and Melanchthon during these early years in Wittenberg before the death of Luther and the frightening defeat of the Schmalkaldic League. While Luther had written positively about Flacius and recommended him as a gifted student and a man of great faith, it was Melanchthon who did the most to advance the Illyrian.[31] As noted already, he took Flacius into his home. He supplemented the education Flacius was receiving in his classes. Their conversations fueled the Illyrian's desire to learn more and more. Melanchthon's approach to academic work, elaborated upon in their time together in the lecture hall and outside of it, molded Flacius' own. His network grew through his teacher and friend. Melanchthon also benefited. He recognized Flacius' talent; surely asked about his experiences in Venice, Basel, and elsewhere; and appreciated his gift for languages. We know that Melanchthon did not keep his fondness for Flacius to himself. He admitted it still later in life, even after all the conflict, as an explanation for why

29 In 1556, Lupetino would die by drowning.

30 Preger, *Matthias Flacius Illyricus und seine Zeit*, 1:24.

31 For examples of Luther's positive assessments and recommendations of Flacius, see Ilić, *Theologian of Sin and Grace*, 63.

Flacius' opposition after the interims stung so much, saying, "I used to enjoy friendship and familiarity with Illyricus." He made it plain with others too, recommending Flacius as one who "surpasses Epiphanius of Salamis who spoke five languages."[32]

It is no wonder that friendship blossomed between the two. They were both eclectic scholars, products of their own personal intuitiveness as much as formal education. They were both historians in their own right, with surprisingly similar approaches to the discipline even before Melanchthon could exert any influence over Flacius, or at least it would seem. Throughout his life, Flacius praised Melanchthon's *Loci communes theologici*. It remained one of his favorite books, if not the favorite, as he praised it even in the heights of his conflicts with Wittenberg and quoted from it often. Just as important, Flacius patterned his own work and style on Melanchthon's even when writing against him.

Luther's Death and the Defeat of the Schmalkaldic League

Luther's death was a devastating event for Wittenberg. While Luther had centered his reform not in himself but in Christ, his personality had helped drive what happened in Wittenberg and beyond. He was the glue that held things together, even when he was mentally or physically unwell or in spiritual anguish. His death was expected (and had been for years), but Wittenberg was truly never ready, and likely never would have been, to lose such a man. That political turmoil and military defeat would come so soon after his departure from this world only compounded things. When needed most, Wittenberg and Evangelical Germany were without Luther's voice. Many turned to Melanchthon to fill the void, an unfair expectation. His relationship with Luther had worked precisely because they were different in so many ways.

---

32 Ilić, *Theologian of Sin and Grace*, 62.

Luther died in Mansfeld, the same German territory in which he had been born. Having gone to settle a dispute about mining, his father's business, he was overcome by his compounding illnesses and, committing his spirit into the hands of his Savior, died. Luther was not a Protestant pope, as much as his opponents might have maligned him as wanting to be, but he was a commanding figure and an unwavering voice who put spine in the German Reformation during its most trying times. He left no obvious successor. There was only one Luther. Those who despised him rejoiced in this.

There were many Lutherans, though, and numerous gifted theologians had been trained in Wittenberg or by others who had attended the university. Wittenberg grew in prominence following Luther's death, because there his colleagues gathered. The mantle of leadership fell upon Philip Melanchthon, fairly or unfairly. Melanchthon had not asked to lead a reformation. None of the surviving Wittenbergers had, and yet they were left with the task. They faced immense pressure. Expectations were high. This only intensified with the events that quickly followed Luther's death. Everything changed in an instant. Luther was dead, and it appeared soon his Reformation would be too, and no one was certain how to overcome this possibility.

The defeat of the Schmalkaldic League truly changed things. In 1546, Holy Roman Emperor Charles V set things in motion. Johann Friedrich of Saxony and Philip of Hesse, the two most important leaders of the Schmalkaldic League, were placed under an imperial ban. War was now inevitable. The university was closed in November 1546, and Flacius moved to Braunschweig with his wife, with Melanchthon's glowing recommendation.[33] At the Battle of Mühlberg in 1547, the league was defeated and Johann Friedrich was captured—a disastrous development. Duke Moritz of Saxony, who had betrayed his fellow Lutherans and his cousin, Johann Friedrich, occupied Wittenberg. Moritz, who would be derided as the "Judas of Meissen" for his treachery, was rewarded with the electoral title and territory, transferred from his defeated cousin. This included the University of Wittenberg, which was reopened in October 1547. Some faculty, including Melanchthon, considered the possibility of service at a new university. Johann Friedrich hoped to start one in Jena. But Melanchthon and others eventually thought better of such a move,

33 See above, p. 21.

considering instead the importance of maintaining the Wittenberg institution where Luther's reform had begun.

Flacius, who was later critical of the failure of his colleagues to remain loyal to their captured prince, returned to Wittenberg in early 1548 with Elizabeth and their first child, also named Matthias. His career was back on track, and it seemed the university was safe, but the relationship between Melanchthon and Flacius would quickly change as political pressure mounted for theological compromise with the demands of the victorious emperor. Flacius was increasingly aware that he did not have the temperament or the lack of scruples a future in Wittenberg under Moritz would require of him. He was ill at ease with the changing climate and with the willingness of his colleagues to play ball so soon after the drastic changes to the political fortunes of Wittenberg and Electoral Saxony. He continued to perform his professional duties well, however, now teaching Greek and continuing his work with Aristotle too.

The Adiaphoristic Controversy

That there were fault lines among the Wittenberg faculty already before Luther's death is now evident. How manifest they may have been before is unclear. Scholars have debated this and will continue to do so. It is clear that before his colleague's death, Melanchthon had already become more moderate in his theology on certain points, for example, regarding free will. With the great reformer gone, this trend intensified even apart from political pressure. Political pressure, however, did intensify the need to compromise for the survival of the university. Melanchthon was not the only one who recognized this or cooperated. Bugenhagen and many others did the same. Nevertheless, it was Melanchthon's willingness to do so that would trouble Flacius the most. As Melanchthon later felt wounded by his mentee's willingness to publicly oppose his theological compromises, Flacius was cut to the heart by his mentor's willingness to forsake what he considered to be central themes of Luther's preaching and teaching, and to do so under state pressure. Flacius was increasingly disappointed that this man he so greatly admired seemingly did not have the stomach of a martyr, whether he was fair in this assessment or not.

Charles V did not intend to waste his victory. He undertook a recatholicizing agenda with the Augsburg Interim as its primary mechanism. The interim was a legal formula intended to reintroduce Roman Catholic ceremonies and, along with them, explicitly and implicitly, Roman Catholic doctrine. Among the things reintroduced were the seven sacraments, transubstantiation, and the jurisdiction of bishops—and thus the papacy—as well as fasts and feasts. The divine service and the church year were thus reshaped. Moreover, the statement on the teaching of justification was vague, leaving out Protestant keywords.

The Augsburg Interim was unsurprisingly met with widespread resistance among Evangelical leaders and churches. Moritz, already known as the "Judas of Meissen," knew his situation was precarious. He had expanded his realm and prestige, receiving electoral lands and the title, but his grip was tenuous. There were threats within and without. His new subjects were not fond of him, and other Protestant rulers were leery. For this reason, he lobbied unsuccessfully against the release of his cousin Johann Friedrich and moved quickly to reassure those of influence in his new lands of his good will. Moritz could not afford to implement the interim in his territories, but he also could not risk upsetting the emperor by doing nothing. His solution was to task the Wittenberg theologians with a compromise proposal he could use. The Wittenbergers strove to focus primarily on ceremonies, but as will be seen, traditional doctrinal formulations were weakened as well. Concerning justification, the proposal posited:

> Although God does not make human creatures righteous through the merit of their own work, which they perform, but through his mercy, freely, without our merit—so that we boast not of ourselves but of Christ, through whose merit alone we are redeemed from sin and made righteous—nonetheless, the merciful God does not deal with human creatures as with a block of wood but draws them in such a manner that their will cooperates, if they are of the age of reason. They do not receive Christ's benefits if the will and heart are not moved by prevenient grace, so that they stand in fear of God's wrath and detest sin.[34]

34 Kolb and Nestingen, *Sources and Contexts of the Book of Concord*, 185.

Vestments became a particular flash point for the people, as the liturgy was how they experienced doctrine most immediately and regularly. Flacius and others who agreed with him—eventually labeled Gnesio-Lutherans or "genuine Lutherans"—vociferously opposed this new proposal out of Leipzig. In a propaganda coup, Flacius popularized it as the "Leipzig Interim," rather than the "Leipzig Proposal." This "interim," rather than the Augsburg Interim, which Melanchthon had opposed and sought to attenuate with this new proposal for Moritz, became the nigh-unforgivable trespass the Gnesio-Lutherans would insist the Wittenbergers had committed. It would lead to all the controversies that followed in all their polemical fierceness. The Leipzig Interim was so offensive precisely because it was prepared not by enemies of the Gospel but by those who previously had proclaimed the Good News and worked to reform the church in accord with it, by mentors, colleagues, and friends. This controversy over supposed adiaphora—as the Wittenberg theologians termed it, the Adiaphoristic Controversy—produced a steady flow of disagreement over the span of decades.

So what is an adiaphoron, and what sort of things are adiaphora? It is almost impossible to understand Flacius' fight against the compromises made by his colleagues and friends without understanding the term. "Adiaphora" is a term borrowed from the Stoics. Bente explains that "ceremonies which God has neither commanded nor prohibited are adiaphora (*res mediae, Mitteldinge*) and *ceteris paribus* (other things being equal) may be observed or omitted, adopted or rejected."[35] Paul addressed adiaphora when he stressed the importance of Christian freedom being exercised in Christian love, and Christian love demanding a defense of Christian freedom. Thomas Aquinas treated the concept, though not the term. Luther used the term in his first published lectures on Galatians: "For to those who believe in Christ whatever things are either enjoined or forbidden in the way of external ceremonies and bodily righteousnesses are all pure, adiaphora, and are permissible, except insofar as the believers are willing to subject themselves to these things of their own accord or for the sake of love."[36] The doctrine of adiaphora thus had an

35 Bente, "Historical Introductions," 109. This appears in Bente's description of the anti-Adiaphorists' position.

36 AE 27:161–62.

established tradition in Christianity as a whole and Lutheranism in particular. The question for the moment was whether the compromises being made in this instance actually dealt with adiaphora, or indifferent matters. Flacius and those who strove with him against the interims insisted they did not. While some of the matters under consideration might have been adiaphora under other circumstances, the Gnesio-Lutherans asserted that such things were no longer adiaphora when foisted upon the church by the state, introduced (or reintroduced) to imply doctrinal unity where there was none, consented to out of fear, or practiced in a way that obscured the Gospel. One can imagine the Gnesio-Lutherans' guttural reaction to the opening of the Leipzig Interim:

> Our concern is based upon our desire to be obedient to the Roman Imperial Majesty and to conduct ourselves in such a way that his Majesty realize that our interest revolves only around *tranquility, peace and unity*. This is our counsel, made in good faith; it is what we ourselves want to serve and promote wherever possible. For in contrast to what some say and write about us—without any basis—our concern and our intention are always directed not toward causing schism and complications, but rather toward *peace and unity*. We testify to that in the very presence of God, to whom all human hearts are known. Our actions will demonstrate that.[37]

In the time leading up to Flacius' departure from Wittenberg, Melanchthon frequently shared reports with him about conferences and proposals. Melanchthon even had Flacius make a copy of a compromise formula on the doctrine of justification drafted at a conference at Pegau. "What treacle," Flacius lamented.[38] Therefore, Flacius was not speculating about developments. He was in the loop, and he feared a "yawning atheism" behind his colleagues' willingness

---

37 Kolb and Nestingen, *Sources and Contexts of the Book of Concord*, 184 (emphasis added).

38 Olson, *Matthias Flacius and the Survival of Luther's Reform*, 99.

to classify their compromises as nothing more than "adiaphora."[39] "Philomela had put the pipe in the sack and was afraid of the hawk," he complained.[40]

Leaving Wittenberg

While still in Wittenberg, and using pseudonyms, Flacius wrote several pamphlets against the Augsburg Interim and subsequent compromises by Lutherans. It was not long, though, before he felt he could no longer remain in the city. For the time being, he left behind Elizabeth, who was pregnant, and set out to find somewhere from which he could, with the assistance of others, continue the struggle for the survival of Luther's Reformation.[41]

Flacius stopped first in Magdeburg. Nikolaus von Amsdorf and other important religious leaders there prevailed upon him to stay, but he demurred. He questioned if he could withstand the siege that they already saw coming for Magdeburg on "smoked bacon and meat, and also salted and dried fish."[42] He was Illyrian, after all, and both the climate and the diet in Magdeburg seemed at odds with his constitution, especially under stress. Eventually, however, after more travel, he decided that Magdeburg was where he belonged because there he found kindred spirits and fervent opponents of the interims. Amsdorf, one of Luther's oldest friends, a resolute and capable theologian, had prepared the city well for the theological struggle ahead. And Flacius was not the only one to have found his way there under Amsdorf's watch. Magdeburg had gathered an impressive reserve of talent. Just as important, the city had skilled printers. Magdeburg was ready for precisely the kind of fight Flacius thought faithful Lutherans needed to put up at this moment: a war of words, theological debate. No one

---

39 Olson, *Matthias Flacius and the Survival of Luther's Reform*, 124.

40 Olson, *Matthias Flacius and the Survival of Luther's Reform*, 118. Some of Melanchthon's supporters referred to him as "Philomela," which means "nightingale" and alluded to his pleasing prose.

41 Thomas Kaufmann, "Matthias Flacius Illyricus: Lutherischer Theologe und Magdeburger Publizist," in *Mitteldeutsche Lebensbilder: Menschen im Zeitalter der Reformation*, ed. Werner Freitag (Cologne: Böhlau, 2004), 183.

42 Kaufmann, "Matthias Flacius Illyricus," 183.

in Magdeburg, as impressive an array of competent theologians as was there, would fight as furiously as Flacius. His output was unparalleled. Thomas Kaufmann notes: "No other figure in the sixteenth century, not even Martin Luther, wrote and published so many pages in so short a time as did Flacius."[43]

Irene Dingel casts helpful light upon Flacius' self-identification with Luther and his struggles, which only increased during these years.[44] Flacius' confession was who he was, not just what he believed. And as who he was, he felt a great kinship with the reformer who had undergone similar trials and been willing to risk all rather than compromise. For this reason, Luther appears again and again in Flacius' writings during this time (and afterward) as "Dr. Martin Luther of blessed memory";[45] "the honorable master and father Martin Luther";[46] the "Reverend Father Martin Luther of pious memory."[47] Flacius also quoted from Luther's lectures, which he had committed to memory.[48]

Flacius reminded his readers that Luther had prevented compromise at Augsburg in 1530, where "some wanted to reconcile Christ and Belial in adiaphora." He argued that "if Dr. Martin had not at that time been on guard, which one sees in his letters, which are now in print, we now through our own wisdom would not even have a trace of the truth among us."[49] Flacius now saw himself playing a similar role, a Luther to the yielding spirit of his former Wittenberg colleagues.[50]

---

43 Thomas Kaufmann, "'Our Lord God's Chancery' in Magdeburg and Its Fight against the Interim," *Church History* 73, no. 3 (September 2004): 576.

44 Dingel, "Flacius als Schüler Luthers und Melanchthons," 77–93.

45 For instance, see Matthias Flacius Illyricus, *Ein vermanung zur bestendigkeit, in bekentnis der warheit, Creutz, und Gebett, in dieser betrübten zeit sehr nützlich und tröstlich* (Magdeburg: Michael Lotter, 1549), Aiv.

46 Johannes Waremundus, "Eine gemeine Protestation," in *Reaktionen auf das Augsburger Interim: Der Interimistische Streit (1548–1549)*, ed. Irene Dingel (Göttingen: Vandenhoeck & Ruprecht, 2010), 162.

47 Matthias Flacius Illyricus, *Quod Hoc Tempore Nulla Penitus Mutatio in Religione sit in gratiam impiorum facienda* (Magdeburg, 1540), A3v.

48 Matthias Flacius Illyricus, *Vermanung Matth. Flacii Illyrici zur gedult und glauben zu Gott, im Creutz dieser verfolgung Geschrieben an die Kirche Christi zu Magdeburg* (Magdeburg: Christian Rödinger, 1551), Aiiv.

49 Flacius Illyricus, *Ein vermanung zur bestendigkeit*, Hiiir.

50 Flacius Illyricus, *Vermanung Matth. Flacii Illyrici*, Ciir.

That Flacius would later ruin his career over a fight about the doctrine of original sin, which came out of a debate about free will, was probably no coincidence. Already Flacius had noted Melanchthon's move toward Erasmus over a concern about human responsibility and his open discomfort with Luther's *Bondage of the Will*, among other things. Luther, then, had driven Flacius to Magdeburg, and from Magdeburg he would do what he was confident Luther would have done: struggle against Melanchthon's moderating tendencies and fight for the Gospel, without compromise and with everything he had.

MAGDEBURG AND RESISTANCE

Thomas Kaufmann writes that Magdeburg "was the most important destination of unrepentant religious emigrants who opposed the politics of the Interim."[1] From the several printing presses within the town's walls came hundreds of documents in opposition to the interims and in resistance to the policies of the emperor. Matthias Flacius fit right in, and he made use of his friends and the printing press. Moritz besieged the city with imperial troops in 1550, but Flacius and his compatriots were determined to stand firm and rally others to their cause.

Magdeburg had an interesting political history that played an important role in how things unfolded during the interim crisis. From the time the Reformation began to make gains in the city, political tensions had been exacerbated. The Reformation was more than simply a religious movement in Magdeburg. The direction taken by the city's resistance to the emperor and his allies represented an assertion of authority by the city council, which had been struggling for independence from the archbishop, who claimed temporal and spiritual authority over the city. With these new developments,

1 Thomas Kaufmann, "Our Lord God's Chancery," 568.

the city council's occupation of the lands of the archbishopric were justified with defensive rationales.[2] This was perhaps necessary but also convenient.

Olson explains that "unlike Nuremberg," which was a free imperial city (and thus subject only to the emperor), "Magdeburg was almost free. . . . So that no one in the city could forget it, there was a forbidding barrier dividing the Altstadt from the Newmarket, which was under the direct rule of the archbishop."[3] This did not mean, however, that the archbishop made claims only on the area under his direct control. He expected fealty from all of Magdeburg. The city council, for its part, hearkened back to privileges granted to it by Emperor Otto I (r. 962–973), its "ancient liberties."[4] Otto held a powerful place in Magdeburg's history, and while these liberties weren't carefully defined, because they were grounded in this part of Magdeburg's past added import to the council's claims. Needless to say, the archbishop had no intention of releasing his claims even as the Reformation occurring within its walls emboldened the city in making its own. Flacius, like so many others, was useful in this cause. Cynicism in this regard must be kept in check, however. The people of Magdeburg did not risk all simply for a stronger council. The Reformation and long-festering debates aligned. Neither negated the other.

Writing Against the Adiaphorists

Flacius followed a basic pattern in his Magdeburg writings. He stated the issues, identified the opponents, and explained what faithfulness looked like. He considered this "an orderly and methodical

2 Thomas Kaufmann, *Das Ende der Reformation* (Tübingen: Mohr Siebeck, 2003), 26–38. See also Nathan Rein, *The Chancery of God: Protestant Print, Polemic and Propaganda against the Empire, Magdeburg 1546–1551* (Burlington, VT: Ashgate, 2008), 58–60, 130–56.

3 Oliver K. Olson, "Theology of Revolution: Magdeburg, 1550–1551," *The Sixteenth Century Journal* 3, no. 1 (April 1972): 62.

4 Olson, "Theology of Revolution," 62.

fashion," and it proved to be so.[5] Flacius laid down a general rule concerning adiaphora:

> All ceremonies and church practices are in and of themselves free, and they will always be. When, however, coercion, the false illusion that they were worship of God and must be observed, renunciation [of the faith], offense, [or] an opening for godlessness develops, and when, in whatever way it might happen, they do not build up but rather tear down the church of God and mock God, then they are no longer adiaphora.[6]

It was clear, Flacius concluded, that none of the purported adiaphora were indeed adiaphora in this context.

One of the chief purposes of Flacius' writings was to urge Christians to stand firm and reject the current compromises, accepting the consequences for doing so. It was a time to heed the Word of God and not human counsel, which had created this mess and continued to make it worse.[7] Peace now risked hell later. Better to suffer in the moment and enjoy heaven forever. What Christians did in this situation would teach others now and for centuries to come: "The eyes of all men are upon us. We must therefore concede nothing at all to the devil nor give any glory to the impious nor stir up disillusion among the weak."[8]

Flacius argued that for ceremonies to be truly indifferent—real adiaphora—three things must be true. First, the church had to choose them freely. Second, they had to spring from proper authorities within the church. Third, they had to stand in keeping with what the Scriptures taught about adiaphora. Thus context mattered. Ceremonies that brought baggage with them, which bore an association with godlessness and had been for that reason done away with, should not be reintroduced. These ceremonies were no longer indifferent. These basic

---

5 Matthias Flacius Illyricus, *Ein buch, von waren und falschen Mitteldingen, Darin fast der gantze handel von Mitteldingen erkleret wird, widder die schedliche Rotte der Adiaphoristen. Item ein brieff des ehrwirdigen Herrn D. Joannis Epini superintendenten zu Hamburg, auch von diesem handel an Illyricum geschrieben* (Magdeburg: Christian Rödinger, 1550), Jiv.

6 Flacius Illyricus, *Ein buch, von waren und falschen Mitteldingen*, Aiv.

7 Flacius Illyricus, *Ein vermanung zur bestendigkeit*, Fiiir.

8 Flacius Illyricus, *Quod Hoc Tempore*, B1r.

principles drove Magdeburg's fight against the Adiaphorists, those who claimed that what was being commanded of the Evangelicals by the emperor or the new elector of Saxony was at its core indifferent, in the realm of that which is neither commanded nor forbidden by God.

The Magdeburg Confession

The Magdeburg Confession has been called the "birth certificate of the Gnesio-Lutheran movement."[9] Although not the author, Flacius' arguments were used amply by the authors (likely Nikolaus Gallus and/or Amsdorf).[10] Kaufmann classifies Flacius as the heart and motor of Magdeburg.[11] His writings represent about 40 percent of Magdeburg publications during this controversy.[12] Flacius did not sign the confession, but there is a very simple reason for that. He was not a pastor but a lay theologian, like Melanchthon. One cannot read the confession, however, without noticing similar themes, references, imagery, and labels from Flacius' earlier writings. The confession also followed a very Flacian order, laid out like so many of his works. It is hard to imagine the Magdeburg Confession existing without him, even though he did not write or sign it.

The Magdeburg Confession has three main parts. At the outset, the right of resistance is stated: "When the higher magistrate is violently persecuting the law itself among his subjects, whether natural law or divine, or the true religion and worship of God, then the lesser magistrate ought to resist him, and this according to God's command." Resistance, the confessors insisted, was appropriate in this circumstance.[13] While Melanchthon had left things up to individual

---

9 Kaufmann, *Das Ende der Reformation*, 176.

10 See Christian Preus, trans., *The Magdeburg Confession: With Historical Introduction and Annotations* (St. Louis: Concordia Publishing House, 2025), especially the introduction by Ryan C. MacPherson, which discusses potential authors and Flacius' influence.

11 Kaufmann, *Das Ende der Reformation*, 177.

12 Kaufmann, *Das Ende der Reformation*, 73.

13 Preus, *Magdeburg Confession*, 45 (cf. *Confessio et Apologia Pastorum & reliquorum ministrorum Ecclesiae Magdeburgensis* [Magdeburg: Michaelem Lottherum, 1550], A1v; *Bekenntnis Unterricht und vermanung der Pfarrhern*

consciences, the Magdeburgers argued that there was a clear biblical mandate.[14] It was probably no coincidence that Melanchthon's funeral oration for Luther was one of the first texts published in German in Magdeburg during the crisis.[15] In that oration, Melanchthon worked hard to encourage people to remain faithful to Luther's message, even in the face of opposition. He succeeded so well that the Magdeburgers used his oration for their cause.

While the first section largely aligns the Magdeburg Confession with the Augsburg Confession, the second part is the most important. It provides the framework for Magdeburg's resistance and the city council's sovereignty. Here the reader finds both theological and legal arguments. Three key developments in Lutheran thought on this topic stand out. The Magdeburg city council was said to have both the right and the duty to defend its subjects against higher authority in this instance, which was an expansion of the realm of divine authority in secular government (it was not reserved only for kings, princes, and emperors). The council's authority came from God, not through the higher authorities. Second, the defense of Magdeburg from tyranny was rooted in the doctrine of vocation. Third, the struggle of the Israelites for freedom from oppression was paradigmatic for all Christians in their struggle against the antichrist.[16] The confessors made clear, however, that this was a defensive struggle. The Magdeburgers had not been looking for a fight; the fight had been brought to them. They wanted nothing other than peace. They offered obedience so long as they could. They argued that resistance was not

---

und Prediger der Christlichen Kirchen zu Magdeburgk [Magdeburg: Michel Lotther, 1550], Aiv).

14 Olson, *Matthias Flacius and the Survival of Luther's Reform*, 91.

15 Nathan Rein, *Chancery of God*, 66. See Melanchthon, *Oration at the Funeral of Dr. Martin Luther*, trans. Christopher Boyd Brown, in *Sixteenth Century Biographies of Martin Luther*, ed. Christopher Boyd Brown, Luther's Works Companion Volume (St. Louis: Concordia Publishing House, 2018), 38–51.

16 Robert von Friedeburg, "Magdeburger Argumentationen zum Recht auf Widerstand gegen die Durchsetzung des Interims (1550–1551) und ihre Stellung in der Geschichte des Widerstandsrechts im Reich, 1523–1626," in *Das Interim 1548/50*, ed. Luise Schorn-Schütte (Gütersloh: Gütersloher, 2005), 429.

a step they wanted to take but one they had to take. They summarized the problem for the emperor:

> These duties of twofold obedience mutually serve and aid each other without offense to conscience on either side and without tumult, so long as each stays within the limits prescribed by God and by the laws that govern their office. But when there is a departure on either side, horrible sins and serious tumults necessarily arise—as you now, Emperor Charles, are exceeding the limits of your kingdom and are extending your kingdom into the kingdom of Christ. Therefore, you yourself are the reason for these disturbances, just as Elijah once said to Ahab. Those are not the cause who will not and cannot, out of fear of God's wrath and eternal punishment, pay to you the honor that you have seized away from God.[17]

The Magdeburgers insisted that God's Word, together with natural and civil law, left them no choice but disobedience under these circumstances. And these circumstances existed because of the emperor's actions.

The third and final part of the confession was aimed at fellow Evangelicals. It argued that there was no room for timidity or neutrality in this cause. It asked how any faithful Christian could supply assistance to the emperor and his attempt to silence the Gospel. It equated such assistance with apostasy and persecution of Christ Himself. There was no middle ground. There were no excuses. The siege of Magdeburg became a stalemate until Moritz and other Lutheran leaders turned on the emperor. The "Judas of Meissen" became the savior of Lutheranism, at least as he and his line would present it. Flacius and others would not let his earlier treachery against Johann Friedrich be forgotten, however, to the great and enduring displeasure especially of Moritz's brother and successor, Augustus.

The Siege Is Broken

What led Moritz to turn on the emperor, for whom earlier he had turned on his fellow Lutherans? Moritz read the wind. Other

17 Preus, *Magdeburg Confession*, 93 (cf. *Confessio*, F1v–F2r; *Bekenntnis*, Jiiv–Jiiir).

Lutheran leaders, who had been assured that the events that led to the defeat of the Schmalkaldic League were only political and would not lead to religious change, quickly realized they had been deceived. As the siege of Magdeburg drew out, and pamphlets flew throughout Germany, it became clear that this was a religious campaign against the Evangelicals. A new military alliance began to take shape, founded on the original confession made by the Evangelicals at Augsburg in 1530 and, increasingly, also aimed at delivering Magdeburg. Moritz found himself in a bind. He could join this alliance, though if it failed, potentially the Lutheran resistance would amplify the "Judas of Meissen" narrative against him even as the emperor's demands as victor would further alienate Moritz from his subjects. Yet if he did not join, and the alliance succeeded without him, he would suffer as an ally of the emperor. Moritz chose to seize the opportunity as best he could. He offered to join the alliance and nominated himself for leadership. Understandably, the other Lutheran leaders were leery. Moritz thus made pledges of loyalty to the Evangelical confession of the faith. He promised to reject any imperial demands that the Lutherans submit to the rulings of the Council of Trent. He also promised to end the military struggle against Magdeburg. The new alliance of Lutheran princes overtook the emperor, and 1552 marked the end of Charles V's hopes of returning his empire to Roman Catholicism. Moritz had won again, but this time his victory brought some breathing room for Lutheranism instead of an existential threat to its future.

Ultimately, like Moritz's earlier duplicity, this alliance was intended "to solidify his rule."[18] Magdeburg and Moritz both declared victory. Magdeburg had never capitulated. It had held out until the very end, tenaciously, and at great cost. Moritz knew this. When he spoke of the end of the siege as a surrender by the city, he was reminded that they had come to terms, and he accepted the correction. Magdeburg's successful war of words had driven home the point that public relations mattered as much as military might (an important sixteenth-century development). As a sign of his benevolence, Moritz guaranteed freedom to Flacius and Gallus, the two most notorious propagandists, surely a pleasant surprise.

---

18 David Mark Whitford, *Tyranny and Resistance: The Magdeburg Confession and the Lutheran Tradition* (St. Louis: Concordia Publishing House, 2001), 89.

Flacius' marketing of Magdeburg's cause, together with those working with him to flood Germany with a call to faithfulness and resistance, had undermined imperial attempts at censorship and won the battle for popular opinion, which was key to the failure of the siege. The Peace of Augsburg of 1555 "recognized the central claim of the Magdeburg pastors and the Torgau Articles—religious diversity does not equal imperial disloyalty."[19] Magdeburg henceforth became synonymous with the defense of Luther's teaching and the rights of the church to govern its preaching and teaching without imperial interference. Led by its eclectic mix of pastors and theologians, including an Illyrian, Magdeburg had made its stand and survived. For that it would pay dearly in the Thirty Years' War.

In late 1551, the Flacius household moved from Magdeburg to Köthen, in Anhalt. Nikolaus Gallus, Flacius' Magdeburg ally and a native son of Köthen (his father was mayor), appears to have arranged things. The reason for the move is unclear, though it is likely that Flacius was concerned about Moritz's sincerity when he guaranteed his freedom. Flacius, after all, had been a thorn in the elector's flesh and had worked feverishly to paint him as a traitor and an illegitimate ruler. There were grounds to suspect the breadth of Moritz's magnanimity. Gallus appears to have been willing to take his chances but understood his friend's desire to find a new home, at least for the time being. While in Köthen, Flacius debated his future. With the controversy over adiaphora settled, what, if any, career was there for him to explore? What was his place in Lutheranism? Should he focus on bookselling? Should he start a school?

In March 1552, Flacius returned to Magdeburg. Olson claims that Melanchthon pressured the prince of Anhalt to expel Flacius from Köthen.[20] Upon his return to Magdeburg, Flacius threw himself into bookselling. During this time, he was a regular at some of the most prominent book fairs in Germany, in person or through intermediaries. He did good business. He had a strong network, impressive knowledge about an array of manuscripts from different disciplines, and an eye for literary treasures. Throughout the doctrinal debates that took place in German Lutheranism during Flacius' remaining time in Magdeburg, he supported himself with bookselling, and it

---

19 Whitford, *Tyranny and Resistance*, 90.

20 Olson, *Matthias Flacius and the Survival of Luther's Reform*, 219.

was to bookselling that he would return during challenging economic periods in the future. In the early 1550s, Duke Johann Albrecht I offered Flacius a Hebrew professorship at the University of Rostock, but he declined the offer.[21]

The Majoristic Controversy

While Magdeburg had emerged from the crisis over the interims intact and uncowed, its theologians had not been vindicated in the eyes of all. Many of the Wittenbergers harbored thinly veiled (if veiled at all) resentments. It was not long until hostilities resumed. Leading Wittenbergers wanted to defend their approach to the interims and protect the reputation of their colleague Melanchthon. Georg Major, one of the contributors to the Leipzig Interim, became, somewhat against his intentions, a leading voice in this camp in what became a dispute over good works. Major himself had considered the Leipzig Interim a "sad, dangerous work."[22] He downplayed his role, claiming to have been a reluctant participant. At the time, his motivation had been more about defending Wittenberg than promoting the proposal from Leipzig. Nevertheless, in defending Wittenberg he had been defending the proposal, whether he liked it or not, because the proposal was the product of the Wittenberg theologians who participated in its development.

Major had been friends with Amsdorf while both were at Wittenberg. Major also had served with Amsdorf in Magdeburg as a school rector for nearly a decade, from 1529 to 1537. The two regularly corresponded after Major returned to Wittenberg. Along with Amsdorf, Major himself had defended Johann Friedrich's military action against the emperor. Open conflict between the two did not appear likely, until Major began to blame the Magdeburgers for the ruptures that developed within Lutheranism over the Adiaphoristic Controversy. When Major moved to Eisleben in 1551 to assume a position as superintendent over the churches, Amsdorf was skeptical. The previous superintendent, Johann Spangenberg, had been a

21 Ilić, *Theologian of Sin and Grace*, 109–10.

22 Preger, *Matthias Flacius Illyricus und seine Zeit*, 1:359.

vocal critic of the Leipzig Interim. It was surprising to have a participant in the interim's creation, then, succeed him. Major's time in Eisleben did not last long; there was tension from the start. The clergy of Mansfeld opposed his appointment. In 1552, around Christmas, upon the return from incarceration of Duke Albrecht, who had been imprisoned with Johann Friedrich since the Schmalkaldic League's defeat, Major was dismissed from office. That Albrecht did not want a supporter of the Leipzig Interim and loyal subject of the treacherous Moritz makes sense. Major thus returned to Wittenberg, where his previous professorship was still open.

Major had a particular loathing for Flacius, it seems. Major spoke ill of him as a foreigner, attempted to discredit him for his lack of ordination (Melanchthon also, it should be noted, was not ordained), and focused his scorn and mockery especially on Flacius as the leader of the motley Magdeburg cohort who had opposed Wittenberg's compromises and acceptance of Moritz. Flacius was stung by the tone of Major's attacks. He thought they had been on good terms before the crises. In fact, Flacius objected that he had done his due diligence even as disagreement broke out, interacting with Major personally, rather than in print. It was neither the first time nor the last that Flacius would feel betrayed by a friend, whether rightly or wrongly.

Preger reminds us that the Majoristic Controversy cannot be understood apart from the Leipzig Interim. It was the interim that moved Major to offer a defense of Wittenberg's positions, and it was the interim that led his opponents to react so swiftly and sternly. They saw in Major's assertion an extension of earlier adiaphorism, a compromising of the truth of God. Preger writes:

> We saw that the position of the Wittenbergers at the time of the interim had already been to some extent foreshadowed by Melanchthon's long-established attitude toward Luther's doctrinal system, evident since the 1530s. The fragments of truth that he was convinced he had found with his critical spirit, constantly investigating things, seemed worth absorbing to some degree. He believed that he could identify many matters of practical importance in Roman teaching whose adoption could begin to heal the painful rift which he saw the church in great danger of suffering.[23]

23 Preger, *Matthias Flacius Illyricus und seine Zeit*, 1:354.

While Major's attacks had begun before the controversy over good works, it was his assertion about good works that blew things wide open. Major was moved in part by a fear of libertinism, that people might think themselves justified apart from repentance. The Wittenbergers had accused the Magdeburgers of antinomianism on more than one occasion. Amsdorf insisted that Major knew full well that they taught correctly in Magdeburg regarding faith and good works.[24] Flacius also dismissed such claims.[25] In defending himself and the Leipzig Interim after the debacle in Eisleben, Major argued that good works are not only necessary, but necessary *for salvation*, and that this distinction was necessary because Christians were taking the Gospel for granted. At least in part, he did so to stave off the purported licentiousness invited by the teaching of the Gnesio-Lutherans. While his statement therefore represented a strategic move in ecclesiastical politics, it also sprang from religious (moral) concerns.

Major's argument that good works are necessary for salvation went beyond what the Leipzig Interim had stated, though it did build upon it. The interim had declared "those works are good and necessary which God has commended"; "good works are necessary, for God has commanded them"; and "new virtues and good works are also most necessary so that, if they are not awakened in the heart, there is no reception of divine grace."[26] None of this went so far as Major would go, but one can see what Major was striving to defend.

In Major's assertion that good works are necessary *for salvation*, the Gnesio-Lutherans found confirmation of what they thought had been hinted at earlier.[27] They understood this as a step toward a Roman scheme of salvation. Amsdorf immediately objected. He argued that "'good works' would be understood by the common people as the works of external performance, not the new obedience which flows

24 Nikolaus von Amsdorf, *Ein kurtzer unterricht auff D. Georgen Maiors Antwort das er nit unschüldig sey wie er sich tragice rhümet* (Basel, 1552), Civr.

25 Matthias Flacius Illyricus, *Bericht M. Fla. Jllyrici, Von etlichen Artikeln der Christlichen Lehr, und von seinem Leben, und enlich auch von den Adiaphorischen Handlungen, wider die falschen Geticht der Adiaphoristen* (Jena: Thomas Rebart, 1559), Hiiir.

26 Kolb and Nestingen, *Sources and Contexts of the Book of Concord*, 189–90.

27 Preger, *Matthias Flacius Illyricus und seine Zeit*, 1:355.

from faith, Major's understanding of the term."[28] Major saw salvation as the product of justification. Amsdorf saw salvation and justification as essentially the same thing, and so reacted swiftly. While Amsdorf overstated his case against Major's formulation, arguing that good works are detrimental to salvation, which also could confuse the laity, this longtime friend of Luther, who had spent a career introducing and preserving the Reformation with and for the great reformer, was right to be uneasy. Major's assertion did more than say that good works are necessary, in that faith without works is dead, as the apostle James insists in his epistle (James 2:17). By adding that good works are necessary "for salvation," Major went too far.

Major thought he was defending Melanchthon's position, but Melanchthon did not recognize it as his own, although he did misrepresent the concerns of Flacius and other Gnesio-Lutherans as antinomianism.[29] As will be seen, Flacius' position was perhaps more Melanchthonian than Melanchthon's own, and Melanchthon was anything but an antinomian. Throughout his reforming career, antinomianism was his great bogeyman; nevertheless, on the relationship between faith and good works, Melanchthon should not be associated with the position Major took. Melanchthon did differ with Luther in his treatment of good works to a degree, but Major's immoderate formula went beyond such divergence. While Luther emphasized the contrast between faith and works—and necessarily so, given the doctrinal battles he fought early in his reforming work—Melanchthon tended to stress the connection between the two, as can be seen in the sixth article of the Augsburg Confession.[30] What Major posited went a step further. In trying to emphasize the connection between faith and works, Major obfuscated the distinction between them in a problematic way.

Flacius was willing to concede that the statement could be understood charitably in the realm of the Law, in that Christ perfectly kept the Law and the Savior's obedience is imputed to the believer through faith, so that the Law is fulfilled for the believer. Lauri

28 Arand, Nestingen, and Kolb, *The Lutheran Confessions*, 191.

29 Arand, Nestingen, and Kolb, *The Lutheran Confessions*, 192.

30 Irene Dingel, "Historische Einleitung," in *Der Majoristische Streit (1552–1570)*, Controversia et Confessio. Theologische Kontroversen 1548–1577/1580: Kritische Auswahledition 3 (Göttingen: Vandenhoeck & Ruprecht, 2014), 3.

Haikola describes Flacius' position regarding the Law and salvation for us: "In matters of salvation, God temporarily dispenses with the requirement of the law. The law has been upheld once and for all [in Christ], so that God is under a sort of obligation to forgive mankind."[31] In other words, Christ's fulfillment of the Law put God in a kind of debt to the Christian. For this reason, the Law had no place in matters of salvation.

By introducing the Law (good works) into matters of salvation, therefore, Major obscured the Gospel by inserting the believer into the salvation equation, a place where the believer must rather be purely passive, receiving eternal life as a gift through faith, which is itself a gift. The Law had its place, but it was not here. The Law had its place even in the life of the believer, but not here. Salvation was and must remain a gift. Flacius was not indifferent to human responsibility, God's immutable will, or new obedience. He emphasized all of these, contrary to the claims of his opponents. Rather, Flacius was insistent that in matters of salvation any room for the Law as a means for contribution by the sinner to redemption was a rejection of Christ's work, which included His perfect obedience, which was the Christian's by imputation and not participation. Here Flacius was much closer to Melanchthon's teaching than to Major's. This fact is seldom appreciated enough by historians and theologians.

The Majoristic Controversy lasted for decades, although Flacius and Amsdorf's victory was evident early in the dispute. Major stopped using the formula that good works are necessary for salvation, but he did not cease defending himself and Wittenberg, even when it meant claiming he never said things he had demonstrably said. He felt he was a victim. When it came to Flacius (and he blamed Flacius particularly for the growth of this dispute and its persistence), Major had less scruples than in dealing with others. For the rest of his life, Major insisted on his orthodox position on the Lutheran doctrine of justification and denied that he had ever veered from it. He even met with Amsdorf in 1563, years after the outbreak of the controversy. The topic of good works, however, did not come up. Major could overlook the opposition of the grandfather of Gnesio-Lutheranism toward his formula, at least for a day. He had, after all, considered Amsdorf his

---

31 Lauri Haikola, *Gesetz und Evangelium bei Matthias Flacius Illyricus* (Lund: Gleerup, 1952), 248.

"dear father and preceptor," as Robert Kolb notes.[32] But there was no such grace for Flacius, who would continue to be the object of Major's abuse—theological, institutional, ethnic, linguistic, and cultural.

The Majoristic Controversy led to another dispute. Justus Menius had opposed the Leipzig Interim but later found himself lumped in with its supporters because of his position on good works. He was driven, like Melanchthon and Major, to some degree by a fear of antinomianism. His position in the debate would eventually cost him his career.

Controversy with Menius

During the time of Johann Friedrich's imprisonment, Amsdorf and Menius had worked together closely to bring the churches of ducal Saxony (the lands Johann Friedrich held after losing the electoral title and the electoral circle around Wittenberg) through the tumultuous period. After his father's death, Johann Friedrich II again tasked Amsdorf and Menius, who was superintendent in Gotha, with ecclesiastical supervision, calling on them to conduct visitations of his lands. Joined by several others, they went to work. The visitation dealt with the moral, doctrinal, and liturgical lives of the churches and their members. While Amsdorf affirmed that new obedience flows from faith, like good fruit from a good tree, so that one can expect such fruits among believers, Menius' position went further. Menius held that the statement that good works are necessary for salvation could be understood correctly, so far as it was understood theoretically and in the doctrine of the Law.[33] In this he was not completely out of line with many former students of Melanchthon. As will be seen, even Flacius was willing to grant this to a certain degree. Amsdorf, however, convinced that Luther would never have countenanced such a statement, objected. Menius' position unsurprisingly was conflated with Majorism. Johann Friedrich II was not happy. The visitations were to bring unity, not division. Reading the tea leaves, Menius fled

---

32 Robert Kolb, *Nikolaus von Amsdorf: Champion of Martin Luther's Reformation* (St. Louis: Concordia Publishing House, 2019), 87.

33 For more on this, see Kolb, *Nikolaus von Amsdorf*, 101ff.

in early 1555, escaping a summons by the duke. He subsequently published works that explained his position. He insisted that new obedience was a necessary part of salvation. Amsdorf was convinced of the danger of Menius' teaching. A synod (meeting of church leaders) was called at Eisenach in August 1556, chaired by Viktorin Strigel, a theologian who, perhaps more than anyone else, would contribute to Flacius' downfall.

At the synod, Menius tried to take a compromising approach. He admitted that his words could be misunderstood by the common people but insisted that they could be understood correctly, theoretically, in the doctrine of the Law. While the synod would affirm that, according to the Law, good works are necessary for salvation (the Law can give salvation only according to works), Menius complained that he had not received a fair hearing and that his position was never truly understood. Amsdorf was unhappy with the synod's concession and dared others to condemn his own position, but nothing came of that. Seven theses were produced by the synod.[34] One, the first, included an admission that the contention that good works are necessary for salvation could be understood correctly in the doctrine of the Law, abstractly, but not concretely. It read: "Even if the statement that good works are necessary for salvation is able to be understood correctly in the doctrine of the Law, abstractly and concerning an idea, there are nevertheless many serious reasons why it should be avoided and fled no less than the statement: Christ is a creature."[35] The synod thus did not encourage the use of such a statement, since it was prone to misinterpretation. Menius signed the theses, although, to his frustration, this did not lead to the restoration of his office. Amsdorf also signed, unhappily. Amsdorf then set to work complaining about the synod to the duke. He considered the synod's distinctions sophistries. One did not preach abstractions, after all.

Here Flacius entered the scene again. Representatives of Johann Friedrich II asked for Flacius' opinion on the theses. Flacius at this

---

34 The opinions of Flacius and Johann Wigand regarding these theses can be found in Matthias Flacius Illyricus, *Matthiae Flacij Illyrici, de voce & re Fidei quodque sola fide iustificemur, contra Pharisaicum hypocritarum fermentum, liber* (Basel: Johannes Oporinus, 1563), 208–18. Flacius provides the theses in the same work, 191–204.

35 Flacius Illyricus, *De voce & re Fidei quodque sola fide iustificemur*, 192.

point had criticized Menius' works, so there was no expectation of impartiality. Flacius and Johann Wigand nevertheless supported the theses, although they made clear that the statement that good works are necessary for salvation should not be used in preaching or in writing—it was just theoretical, an idea, that could be understood only in the doctrine of the Law. For once, Flacius and Amsdorf found themselves on opposite sides of a theological debate. The disagreement remained civil, however. Whether it gave Amsdorf pause, we do not know, but he did persist in his opposition to the theses of the synod, particularly the concession that good works could be considered necessary for salvation abstractly in the doctrine of the Law. Here Amsdorf was more Luther's disciple and Flacius more Melanchthon's. They went back and forth for quite some time about the issue, with Flacius and Wigand insisting that the Law of Moses made clear that good works were necessary for salvation *according to the Law*. The question for them was not whether good works contributed to salvation as sinners actually received it—passively, through faith, as a gift apart from merit and for Christ's sake alone—but whether according to the Law good works were necessary, if the Law should grant anyone salvation. While Amsdorf feared the thesis confused the biblical teaching on righteousness (that is, the righteousness that avails before God), Flacius and Wigand were concerned with upholding "the Creator's will and unchangeable order."[36] For them, this was a matter of properly distinguishing Law and Gospel. In defending the Gospel, one ought not do violence to the doctrine of the Law. The Law did deal in active righteousness, and it did express the immutable will of God. It was said of the Law that those who do it will live.[37] This did not imply an ability for a sinner to keep the Law, but it was nonetheless what was promised regarding the Law, impossible as it was for fallen people. Just as a rose is a flower, much cherished in the summer but nowhere to be found in the winter, so after the fall Christians who can perfectly keep the Law are nowhere to be found.[38] Christ, nevertheless, had perfectly fulfilled the Law as the God-man—not as a creature, but as the Creator in the flesh. His obedience was perfect and crucial. This was not inconsequential for our salvation. Christ gave

36 Arand, Kolb, and Nestingen, *The Lutheran Confessions*, 195.

37 See Leviticus 18:5; Galatians 3:12.

38 Flacius, *De voce & re Fidei quodque sola fide iustificemur*, 193.

salvation as a gift precisely because He had fulfilled the Law, which made such a necessary gift possible on God's behalf. Christ's obedience, as well as His righteousness, was imputed to the believer.

Kolb explains that the dispute between the men came to an end when Amsdorf asked Flacius to stop writing him about the controversy. Recognizing the importance of retaining Amsdorf's friendship, Flacius "begged Amsdorf not to condemn him. He thanked his reverend father in the Lord for treating him with singular Christian kindness, and he asked for Amsdorf's guidance and correction."[39] Despite the conciliatory tone, Amsdorf doubted their positions were in agreement.

The two appear to have remained on good terms. It should be noted that Flacius made his arguments concerning good works and the Law while at a point of particular prominence as a Lutheran theologian. As he brought the discussion to a close, he certainly did so not only to remain in Amsdorf's favor, but also he surely felt a deep affection for the older man and did not want to lose a cherished friendship. The response was not merely self-serving, though. Flacius did not want unnecessary dissension among the Gnesio-Lutherans, and he respected Amsdorf's concerns—both men recognized the danger of preaching such a proposition concretely. That he was willing to be deferential and essentially sue for peace runs counter to narratives that Flacius was a controversialist who was by nature eager to win a debate at any cost or indifferent to the divisions caused by disagreements. In fact, his willingness to debate such things testifies for his desire for unity, a unity that, in his view, came from struggle together for the truth—honest dialogue—rather than ambiguity or a fear of disputation about the things of God.

The Osiandrian Controversy

The Majoristic Controversy was not the only dispute Flacius took part in during his time in Magdeburg after the end of the siege. He played a prominent role in the Osiandrian Controversy as well. While Flacius saw Major's position on good works as an indirect but dangerous

39 Kolb, *Nikolaus von Amsdorf*, 112–13.

attack on the doctrine of justification by grace through faith alone, the Osiandrian Controversy involved a direct attack upon Luther's doctrine of justification. Andreas Osiander the Elder (1498–1552) rejected Luther's forensic justification and Melanchthon's emphasis on imputation, instead emphasizing indwelling, or infusion, in his teaching on justification. In doing so, Osiander aroused opposition from practically every corner of post-Luther Lutheranism. The Osiandrian Controversy, in fact, became an unintentionally ecumenical endeavor. Bitter opponents found themselves united in opposition to Osiander's teaching.

Andreas Osiander had impressive Reformation credentials. He had been a student of Melanchthon's great-uncle, Johann Reuchlin, who had shaped him as a humanist and exposed him to Hebrew. Later he would write in defense of the Jews, debunking claims of Jewish conspiracies against Christians, such as blood libel. A gifted preacher, Osiander wielded significant influence in Nuremberg after his arrival and was instrumental in coordinating the reform of the city. He became a close ally of Luther's, one who had not gone out from Wittenberg but had arrived at his conclusions without the direct influence of Luther and Wittenberg, although with the help of their writings.

Osiander left Nuremberg because of his opposition to the Augsburg Interim, and Albrecht of Brandenburg took him in, having been won to the Reformation by Osiander. As duke of Prussia, Albrecht appointed Osiander a pastor in Königsberg. Osiander also lectured at the new university, but from the beginning his relationship with the faculty was tenuous. Osiander had a lifelong interest in the Old Testament and mysticism, especially as filtered through Neoplatonic Jewish mysticism. While his views on justification likely differed from Luther's from the beginning, these differences did not become known publicly until after the reformer's death. Now with the court's protection, Osiander felt emboldened. He opposed the Leipzig Interim but also began to speak more openly about his teaching on justification. When he published on the matter, controversy erupted. Throughout 1551, opposition mounted. Some Gnesio-Lutherans were quick to denounce Osiander's views, Martin Chemnitz among them. Some Wittenbergers, too, did not grant Osiander the benefit of the doubt, given his harsh critique of the Leipzig Interim. Flacius entered the fray as well. Here, after all, was as direct an attack on Luther's message of the Gospel as one could imagine, one aimed squarely at the central teaching of Luther's reform.

What did Osiander teach about justification? It is hard to be precise because Osiander was not. Basically, he taught that sinners were made righteous. That may not sound very different from Luther's teaching, but Osiander taught that sinners were *made* righteous rather than *declared* righteous. He explained that God came to dwell in sinners, and as He did so, the believer became righteous. Righteousness was infused, or poured into, the believer, and it swallowed up sin.[40] Osiander thus attacked both Luther's forensic righteousness and Melanchthon's imputed righteousness. For Osiander, the righteousness taught by Luther and Melanchthon was fake righteousness, not the essential righteousness of Christ's divine nature, and thus it was stony and ineffectual. To many Lutherans, this smacked of the Roman teaching of justification and Roman critiques of Luther's proclamation. Tellingly, some Roman Catholic opponents indeed saw in it a potential opening for dialogue.

As a fellow active opponent of the interims, Osiander had reason to see Flacius as a potential ally in the disagreement that broke out over his position on justification. His writing was sent to Flacius by Duke Albrecht via Magdeburg. Olson notes that Osiander had "already claimed Flacius' approval in print," either without care for the truth or because he was so confident he would receive it.[41] The prospect of the bishopric of Samland was held out, in addition to other potential gifts, should the duke secure Flacius' support in this matter.[42] To Osiander's disappointment, as well as that of Albrecht, support was the last thing Flacius intended to give in this dispute over justification. He was unwilling to break with Luther's teaching, which had brought him so much comfort in his spiritual distress. Flacius said that he would rather make common cause for the truth with the Wittenbergers, who were then his most hostile enemies, then work against it with Osiander, his friend.[43] Once again, Flacius was bound

40 Olson, *Matthias Flacius and the Survival of Luther's Reform*, 286.

41 Olson, *Matthias Flacius and the Survival of Luther's Reform*, 287.

42 Olson, *Matthias Flacius and the Survival of Luther's Reform*, 287; Ilić, *Theologian of Sin and Grace*, 41.

43 Preger, *Matthias Flacius Illyricus und seine Zeit*, 1:218.

to lose a friend because he felt bound to the truth of Scripture as he understood it.

Duke Albrecht was confused. He could not understand how Flacius could choose to side with those who had opposed him so vehemently rather than one who had struggled with him throughout Lutheranism's great existential crisis. He was not the first to be confused in such a way by the Illyrian, and he would certainly not be the last. The duke assumed Flacius must not have understood what Osiander was teaching and held out hope that the two would eventually reconcile. Flacius was not confused, however. He saw Osiander's teaching as a serious threat to the Gospel and biblical Christology. In his writings against his former ally, he restated this threat clearly, summarizing Osiander's teaching perhaps more clearly than had Osiander himself.

In 1552, Flacius and Nikolaus Gallus published their first public blast against Osiander.[44] They wasted no time getting to the point:

> Our righteousness, through which we ourselves become righteous and children of God in this life, acceptable to Him, is the fulfillment of the Law of God. We have not achieved this fulfillment. Christ, true God and man, has achieved it through His perfect obedience, doing all the Law requires of us and suffering that which we should have suffered on account of our sins. This righteousness is given to us by faith, imputed to us, just as if we ourselves had suffered and done everything ourselves.[45]

Here again we seen Flacius as a student of Melanchthon as well as Luther. Here again, as in the debate with Major, we see Flacius' position rooted and framed in terms closer to Melanchthon than to Luther. Divine justice had been met in Christ through His obedience to the Law. Righteousness was earned by Christ and was a gift from Christ. The Christian had no righteousness that avails before God but Christ's, and this the Christian had through faith, by imputation. Flacius throughout his life held fast Luther's dying confession: faith

---

44 Matthias Flacius Illyricus and Nikolaus Gallus, *Verlegung des Bekentnis Osiandri von der Rechtfertigung der armen sünder durch die wesentliche Gerechtigkeit der Hohen Maiestet Gottes allein* (Magdeburg: Rödinger, 1552).

45 Flacius and Gallus, *Verlegung des Bekentnis Osiandri*, Aiv.

was but a "beggarly hand."[46] And what faith received was the righteousness of Christ, unearned and complete, credited not poured.

Other works would follow, all similar in their careful dissection of Osiander's statements and blunt rejection of his teaching of justification, with reasons exhaustively listed. Flacius, who had hoped to settle down and write less, or at least claimed so at the time, was now busy doing work he felt others were neglecting. Perhaps, though, some saw little need, since his pen never rested. In the end, Osiander found little support. His grand hopes were dashed. His opponents proved more imposing than he imagined and his case less convincing. To the duke's disappointment, his beloved theologian, the man who had brought him into Lutheranism, turned out to be out of step with both Wittenberg and Magdeburg.

> Thus, Luther's students rallied against Osiander, whatever other differences they may have had with one another. Righteousness is bestowed by the pronouncement of God, which creates the reality of the forgiven and righteous believer out of the old sinful self. This pronouncement is possible because the whole person of Christ, God and human creature, has been obedient to his Father. In this obedience he has taken sin into his own death and restored life through his resurrection. Righteousness rests in the relationship of the loving Father and his reconciled children, not in anything "ontological" in either a Platonic or Aristotelian sense. Reality is established by the Word of the Lord.[47]

Controversy with Schwenkfeld

The debates erupting from the interims and developing still after the conclusion of the siege of Magdeburg cut right to the heart of Lutheran theology. Disagreements about purported adiaphora led to disputes about justification and good works—things Luther had addressed from the very beginning of his reform, teachings on which there had

46 Matthias Flacius Illyricus, *Breves Summae Religionis Iesu Christi, & Antichristi* (Magdeburg: Michael Lotter, 1550), A4r. Cf. a note Luther wrote shortly before his death: "We are beggars. That is true" (AE 54:475).

47 Arand, Kolb, and Nestingen, *The Lutheran Confessions*, 195.

been assumed unity for decades. The next debate Flacius joined was no less central, dealing with Scripture itself and the Christian's relationship with it. This debate was not a debate within Lutheranism but involved an outsider whose teachings had nevertheless made some inroads in Lutheranism or posed the risk of doing so. Flacius' opponent now was Caspar von Schwenkfeld, a Silesian spiritualist.

Schwenkfeld had experienced some sort of conversion or awakening in the late 1510s. He was influenced by Luther's writings and came to consider himself as an Evangelical early in the Reformation, but the extent to which he was ever a conventional Lutheran is unclear. He began preaching in 1521 and soon won disciples who gathered in conventicles (secret meetings). By 1525, he had rejected the real presence in the Lord's Supper, which would be part of a continuing trend away from the external to the internal, the objective to the subjective.

Schwenkfeld increasingly taught innovative, and heretical, Christology, claiming that while Christ had two natures, human and divine, He had slowly become more divine. All of this alienated Schwenkfeld from mainstream Protestantism. His time in magisterial (official) reform was thus limited, and many scholars today consider him a radical reformer. His rejection of infant Baptism in practice, if not entirely in principle, fits this narrative. Nevertheless, Schwenkfeld's thought is difficult to classify too neatly.

Flacius followed Luther and referred to Schwenkfeld as "Stenkfeld" (think of a freshly manured field in spring) in the polemics that ensued. Flacius saw in Schwenkfeld the unfettered enthusiasm that Luther had so often warned about, *Schwärmerei*, the same trickery of the devil by which Adam and Eve fell, setting themselves above the spoken Word of God. Interestingly, Schwenkfeld had been to Wittenberg twice to attempt to win Luther to his ideas but had been unsuccessful. He did not give up, however, and so as Schwenkfeld's influence rose after Luther's death, Flacius felt compelled to oppose him. Faced with spiritual exegesis, Flacius asserted that such an approach fits Scripture like a fist fits an eye.[48] In Flacius' view, Schwenkfeld erred especially by separating God from His means of grace and true faith from God's external revelation, emphasizing instead inner revelation.[49]

---

48 Olson, *Matthias Flacius and the Survival of Luther's Reform*, 302.

49 Matthias Flacius Illyricus, *Von fürnemlichem stücke punct oder artikel der Schwenkfeldischen schwermerey* (Magdeburg: Michael Lotter, 1553), Aiv–Aiir.

While Flacius took issue with all the unorthodox teachings noted above, his debate with Schwenkfeld focused especially upon Christ as the Word, the external Word (written and especially preached), and the Christian's relationship to the same. Years into the debate and while teaching at Jena, Flacius compiled fifty errors taught by Schwenkfeld. The fiftieth error captured the disagreement well: "That God does not act or deal with us through external means."[50] Years earlier, Flacius had summarized it similarly. Schwenkfeld, he explained, taught "that the Holy Scriptures are not the Word of God" and "that faith does not come from hearing or writing, nor grow through it, nor cling to it," but rather "the true and living faith is not based on the Holy Scriptures, but rather the Holy Scriptures must conform to faith."[51] Flacius' protracted back-and-forth with Schwenkfeld is hardly surprising, therefore. Again, Flacius saw a direct attack on Luther's teaching and the consolation of the sinner, whose faith would only find certainty in the objective promises of God's Word and true meaning in its plain teachings.

In the same way Luther dealt with Erasmus in *Bondage of the Will*, Flacius defended the clarity of Scripture. He insisted it was authoritative and trustworthy, the means through which God spoke to us still today, brought us to faith, and kept us in the same. Christians were to gladly hear and learn this Word. This was an act of the mind as well as the heart. The Christian stood under this Word, not over it, and it spoke from without to within, cutting to the very heart and soul, creating a new heart. The movement was from external to internal, and not vice versa. There was no room for an inner light in the presence of the Light of the world. The Spirit was active in and through the Word, written and preached, administered in the Sacraments, and God had bound Himself to no other means. God had not promised to act in such a way anywhere else. It was in Word and Sacrament where

---

He expanded his critique in *Etliche Contradictiones . . . des Stenckfeldts daraus sein Geist leichtlich kan geprüfet warden* (Nürnberg: Johann vom Berg & Ulrich Neuber, 1556).

50 Matthias Flacius Illyricus, *Funffzig grobe Irthumen der Stenckfeldischen Schwermerey / aus seinen eigen Büchern trewlich zusamen gelesen und verzeichnet / damit sich die einfeltigen Christen desto fleissiger für seinem Giffschewen und hüten* (Jena: Thomas Rebart, 1558), Dir.

51 Matthias Flacius Illyricus, *Von der h. Schrifft vnd jrer wirckung, widder Caspar Schwenckfeld* (Magdeburg: Michael Lotter, 1553), Aiir.

one found a gracious God. This was the only way God had promised to deal with sinners. The Spirit and the letter were not in opposition; the Spirit worked through the letter.

Schwenkfeld had attacked the very foundation and font of Christian life and truth, mercy and grace. Like Erasmus earlier, although in a much more pronounced way, Schwenkfeld undermined the certainty essential to pastoral care and the spiritual health of the Christian. His theology could not preach. It led sinners to their own imaginations and persons rather than to the person of Christ. Flacius knew such enthusiasm could not end well for those drawn into it. He did not become a father of Protestant hermeneutics by leaving the Word up for personal interpretation or subject to inward, unrooted faith. The Christian, he insisted, must hold diligently to the Word of God and the Sacraments.[52] This was God's will, and not opinion. He compiled proofs from Scripture, lest there be doubts. These focused especially on preaching. He knew well the Christian's need for a preacher. It was Lupetino's proclamation of the Gospel that had started him on his journey north, toward Wittenberg. It was Luther's Evangelical consolation from God's Word that had freed him from spiritual darkness and brought him to the Light, Jesus Christ.

The Catalogus

Flacius knew there had been preachers in every age. God had always made sure the Gospel was proclaimed, even if only a remnant listened. It was with this conviction that, in 1552, Flacius undertook one of his most important works, which together with the *Magdeburg Centuries* would cement him as a father of Protestant historical theology. First published in 1556 in Basel by his friend Johannes Oporinus, Flacius' *Catalogus testium veritatis* was an ambitious enterprise and marked an important step in the development of the modern discipline of church history.[53] A 1562 edition followed. The work sought to collect testimonies from church fathers that supported Protestant teaching

---

52 Flacius, *Von der h. Schrifft*, Miv.

53 Matthias Flacius Illyricus, *Catalogus testium Veritatis, Qui ante nostram aetatem reclamarunt Papae: Opus uaria rerum, hoc praesertim tempore scitu dignissimarum, cognitione refertum, ac lectu cum primis utile atq[ue] necessarium* (Basel: Johannes Oporinus, 1556).

and undermined Roman ecclesiastical authority. It was an impressive feat. The second edition had more than four hundred witnesses. Roughly eighty were devoted to the early church. Medieval witnesses received extended attention. Flacius made good use of the Investiture Controversy, the great conflict between Emperor Henry IV and Pope Gregory VII over who should appoint bishops. The incident highlighted for him an important stage in the tyranny of the papacy.[54]

The *Catalogus* had a twofold goal. First, Flacius aimed to show that Christ was the beating heart of the Scriptures, their sum and scope, and that Christian preachers and teachers had recognized this throughout church history, if only a small minority at times. Second, he sought to demonstrate that the papacy was the antichrist and had been recognized as such long before Luther. He began with a study of St. Peter. Luther's teaching, not the pope's, was in line with Peter's teaching. In this way, Luther was more a successor of Peter than any recent pope. Following Peter's entry came a long list of church fathers. Flacius, in contrast to the approach of Reformed scholars, sought to demonstrate continuity in the church. Christ had always had His confessors. The Gospel had always been proclaimed and heard. Yes, sometimes this had been muted. Yes, sometimes the number of such confessors had been small. Yes, sometimes few had heard. Yet the church had never disappeared, nor had the Good News. This emphasis on continuity and remnant theology, which was also pronounced in his writings during the Adiaphoristic Controversy, played a prominent role in Flacius' theology throughout his life, but especially as he faced growing opposition as he aged.

Flacius seems to have savored the opportunity to contrast the positions of the Roman Church of his day with those of the apostles and church fathers. He noted that the popes wanted to build their ministry on Peter's but neglected to acknowledge the apostle's shortcomings and mistakes, even as they appropriated the supposed power and glory as successor to his seat.[55] Flacius was not denigrating Peter. Rather, he was arguing that Peter, aware of his own humanity and humble in his apostolic ministry, would not have recognized those who claimed to be his heirs. Flacius drew several lessons from Scripture's portrayal of Peter's person and ministry. In addition, he

---

54 Flacius, *Catalogus testium Veritatis,* 204ff.

55 Flacius, *Catalogus testium Veritatis,* 2.

pointed out that neither Peter himself nor Paul seemed to acknowledge any Petrine primacy, since Paul rebuked Peter openly at Antioch and Peter accepted the rebuke without asserting any authority beyond that of the Word. Moreover, when Paul warned the Corinthians about divisions in the church, as some were claiming privilege because of the specific pastor or apostle (Peter or Paul) they followed, Paul dismissed all such thinking and mentioned no primacy among these ministers.[56] Flacius' point was clear: the new teaching in the church was not Protestant rejection of papal primacy; rather, papal primacy was the innovation, something the man they claimed to have been the first pope would not have recognized, something that Paul would have condemned.

The *Catalogus* left an important impression upon Protestant church history. It was used and adapted by heirs of the Swiss Reformations and in England. Lutherans continued to use it for quite some time. It sparked an interest in medieval history among Protestants. Perhaps there was more Evangelical history than previously suspected. Moreover, the study of history gained momentum as an essential field of the theological discipline. The notion of a succession of teaching, rather than persons, gained clout. A church's catholic or ancient roots took on more than institutional dynamics. In fact, the church as institution became a more complicated matter. On what was the institution grounded? In whom was it grounded? How was one to recognize the true church, the one that went back to Peter, to Christ? Flacius gave a Protestant, an Evangelical, answer that had staying power. The *Catalogus* also gave birth to innumerable streams of research. Ambitious young scholars, Protestant and Roman Catholic, found all sorts of leads to follow. The *Catalogus* became a search engine of sorts. Whether wanting to dig deeper into its arguments or eager to counter them, theologians and historians discovered angles to explore, rabbit holes to dive into, and manuscripts to chase down, authenticate, and annotate.

---

56 Flacius, *Catalogus testium Veritatis*, 3.

The Magdeburg Centuries

Preger notes that "the Reformation needed to justify itself in two ways: scripturally and historically."[57] Flacius was determined to do both thoroughly, and so on the heels of the *Catalogus* and before working on the *Clavis,* his great hermeneutical work, he undertook the most ambitious project of his career. Flacius began organizing a plan and seeking support for this endeavor in 1553. The *Ecclesiastica Historia,* better known as *Magdeburg Centuries,* was an enormous undertaking. Its first volume, covering the first three centuries of the church, was published in 1559, with the publication of volumes continuing until 1574. It was the most comprehensive history of the church since Eusebius. It marked a conscious break with the hagiographical approach to church history that predated it. Flacius recognized that many lives of the saints lacked historical accuracy and sought to build the *Centuries* around primary sources. Moreover, just as he had argued for apostolic succession in doctrine, not ordinations (which, again, often lacked real historical attestation), an emphasis of the *Centuries* was the demonstration of the continuity of doctrine from antiquity to Protestantism. He focused not so much on great men, saints or other heroes, but on the church itself, using the best manuscripts at his disposal, and he worked tirelessly to increase that number through his network with the support of patrons.[58]

This was too much for one man to do alone. Flacius recruited a team and created guidelines for their work. In so doing, he gave birth to Protestant church history and left an indelible mark on the modern field of historical theology. With financial support acquired, a plan set, and a group of dedicated colleagues in place who believed in the project, its approach to the past, and its artifacts, work began, century by century, rather than following the *Lokalmethode,* which focused on topics or themes. Flacius did appreciate this method, learned from Melanchthon, for systematic theology and had often

---

57 Preger, *Matthias Flacius Illyricus und seine Zeit,* 2:414.

58 For more on the work's aim and the plans and methods underlying it, see Heinz Scheible, *Die Entstehung der Magdeburger Zenturien: Ein Beitrag zur Geschichte der Method,* Schriften des Vereins für Reformationsgeschichte 183 (Gütersloh: Gerd Mohn, 1966).

praised his teacher's use of it. For this project, however, he wanted to work chronologically. This was not periodization, however. They did not proceed in such a way because they thought each century was a natural unit, with a clean narrative that had a clear beginning and end, but they did so simply because it offered a manageable way to organize and publish the hefty volumes that resulted from this massive undertaking.

Flacius' original team, called the Centuriators of Magdeburg, or Collegium, consisted of Johann Wigand, Matthaeus Judex, Martin Copus, Abdias Praetorius, and Marcus Wagner. All had been involved in Magdeburg's resistance to the interims. Others would join the project along the way. The contributors divided up key roles (collecting, organizing, and writing) and agreed on methods in 1556. Flacius did not do much of the writing, but he was the leading mind and the engine. He was more like a baseball manager than a football quarterback. Wigand called Flacius the project's "skipper or supreme helmsman."[59] Scholars have debated what exactly Flacius wrote, and will continue to do so, but in the end what matters is that only Flacius could have gotten such an operation off the ground with the vision, discipline, and confessional integrity it maintained. The *Magdeburg Centuries* simply would not have been—and certainly would not have been what they became—without Flacius. The Illyrian thus left an unmistakable stamp upon German Protestantism. Even more, he molded church history as a whole and the modern discipline of history in general. His imprint is clear.

Roman Catholic apologists often emphasize the deep historical roots and continuity of the Roman Church. This has appealed to many modern North American evangelicals, who recognize the rootlessness of many of their congregations and practices. Flacius and his Protestant colleagues, however, revolutionized the historical discipline and insisted that real history, history rooted in authentic texts, told a different story. Moreover, they argued that continuity rested in teaching, and it was found precisely in the Evangelical churches of the Augsburg Confession. Theirs were churches with established roots. Historical theology was born and grew in its importance as a field. The Centuriators made plain that Luther had not pointed forward, to something new, but had pointed back to the prophets and apostles,

59 Preger, *Matthias Flacius Illyricus und seine Zeit*, 2:424.

reclaiming a full-throated proclamation of the Good News of Jesus Christ. The churches of the Augsburg Confession were not innovative. They were catholic.

Post-Controversy Conversations

As time passed and the Peace of Augsburg came, Flacius hoped unity could be restored within Lutheranism. There was movement by the Hanseatic cities toward this end as they sought to foster inter-Lutheran dialogue. With such talks in mind, Flacius and Gallus had already published a work several years earlier, treating what would need to be discussed and resolved for lasting unity.[60] Five key points of contention needed agreement. First, was the pope the true Antichrist, along with his company, as had been taught in Lutheran churches, and should that truth still be confessed? Second, could there be similarity of ceremonies between the churches of the Augsburg Confession and the Antichrist, his bishops, and the enemies of Christ without idolatry, without denial of and harm to the religion of Christ? Third, was it biblically permissible for secular authorities to institute church orders and ceremonies in the church contrary to the will of the church and good order? Fourth, was it a confusion of the Word of God to cause Christ's Church to introduce practices and ceremonies to please the godless and persecutors of the truth for the sake of bodily peace? Fifth, did those who introduced or submitted to the Leipzig Interim, as its opponents had named it, act in an unchristian manner in their approach, and was resistance instead required during the crisis?[61]

In September 1556, Flacius and Melanchthon corresponded briefly. Flacius asked Melanchthon to confess his errors in the interim crisis. Melanchthon did recant in a letter to Flacius.[62] Flacius was

60 Matthias Flacius Illyricus and Nikolaus Gallus, *Provocation oder erbieten der Adiaphorischen sachen halben, auff erkentnis vnd vrteil der Kirchen* (Magdeburg: Michael Lotter, 1553).

61 Flacius and Gallus, *Provocation oder erbieten*, Aivr–Aivv.

62 Olson, *Matthias Flacius and the Survival of Luther's Reform*, 302; see Karl Gottlieb Bretschneider and Heinrich Ernst Bindseil, eds., *Corpus Reformatorum, Philippi Melanthonis opera quae supersunt omnia*, 28 vols. (Braunschweig: Schwetschke & Sons, 1834–60), 8:841f.

not content with this, however, because it was not a public confession. Melanchthon had already confessed to Bugenhagen and been absolved, but, again, that was a private not public confession. Flacius thought only a public confession could help heal the rifts that had arisen because of the Adiaphoristic Controversy. No such confession was forthcoming. Flacius had endured years of mockery and scorn from Wittenberg. Melanchthon, Bugenhagen, and others had accused him of murderous plots, heresy, and treachery. He had been the victim of ethnic slurs and cutting parody. Perhaps this played into Flacius' insistence on a public confession. Given his track record, however, it seems more likely that he thought public error needed to be publicly addressed for real concord to be restored. Either way, no such unity was imminent, although attempts were being made. These attempts broke down when clashes between personalities and about procedure made any meaningful progress impossible.

The anonymously composed 1557 "Synod of the Birds," attributed to both Johann Major and Melanchthon by scholars, marked a fitting end to attempts at rapprochement.[63] This satirical poem, written in praise of the Wittenbergers and mockery of their opponents, especially those involved in the aforementioned attempts to negotiate new religious peace, paid special tribute to Flacius, the "cuckoo." (Gallus earned the role of the rooster.) The cuckoo, an outsider, lurks, hiding like a nocturnal predator in the brambles, eager for prey, and yet waiting for the moment when his victims are most vulnerable, attacking newborn birds to the dismay of their parents, who love them.[64] This was hardly a subtle dig at the Illryian, who had attacked fellow students of Melanchthon and distressed his teacher, a teacher who had loved and cared for him.

July 17, 1556, brought the prospect of a change for Flacius and his family. He was issued a call to Jena by Duke Johann Friedrich II. This invitation promised prominent roles. Flacius would serve as general superintendent, overseeing the superintendents, pastors, and other

63 *Synodus Avium Depingens Miserum Faciem Ecclesiae propter Certamina Quorundam, Qui de Primatu contendunt, cum oppressione recta meritorum* (n.p., 1557). Regarding the poem and its authorship, see Manfred P. Fleischer, "Melanchthon as Praeceptor of Late-Humanist Poetry," *Sixteenth Century Journal* 20, no. 4 (Winter 1989): 571.

64 *Synodus Avium*, B2r.

church workers of all the churches in the duke's lands. As general superintendent, he would work to make sure no new teachings sprang up in the churches. He would also ensure that only proper ceremonies were observed. In addition, he would teach at the university, founded as a result of the Ernestine loss of Wittenberg to Moritz. Flacius would lecture in Greek and Latin, teaching the New Testament. This was an opportunity to serve the Ernestine line, which he had supported after Luther's death and throughout the Adiaphoristic Controversy. Even more, this was a chance to work for doctrinal orthodoxy and uniformity in Saxony, in the heartland of the German Reformation. He would be back in the classroom too. It is easy to see how attractive this call must have been. Around the same time, Flacius received an invitation to teach at Heidelberg. This, too, was a prominent position in the church and school there. Flacius may well have been tempted, but he kept the commitment he had already made to ducal Saxony. These calls demonstrate that Flacius was still situated within the Lutheran mainstream, respected, with a generally positive reputation. Riding high, then, Flacius set off for what he likely thought would be new heights, toward better days, both for himself and for genuine Lutheranism in Germany.

JENA AND THE PROMISE OF BETTER DAYS

Toward a Life in Perpetual Motion

One might wonder if Jena was predestined to be a university for the idiosyncratic and misfits. This institution Flacius was called to help supervise and grow would later be home to some of Germany's most interesting professors or students, men such as Fichte, Hegel, and Marx. Flacius arrived at an important time. Jena was still an academy when he received the call to join its faculty in 1556. The emperor granted the status of "university" to the Ernestine princes in August 1557, with its inauguration February 2, 1558. The sons of Johann Friedrich I had collected an eclectic mix of sharp minds to fulfill his dream of a university to replace (and rival) Wittenberg, which he had lost as a result of his defeat at Mühlberg. With these sharp minds, though, came strong personalities.

Upon Flacius' arrival, before he had said or done anything in the city, there was tension, which would only grow, especially among the faculty, who competed for the duke's favor and worked to sour him on their rivals. Johann Friedrich II wanted peace and had gathered men he thought would bring it, but in return he received more grief than he could have expected. Flacius did not create this situation, but he did walk into it, and he and his fellow Gnesio-Lutherans contributed to it. As an example of their zeal, Flacius was instrumental in the dismissal of Paul Luther, the reformer's son, as a professor of medicine because of concerns about his theological convictions.[1] Flacius and those of like mind already at Jena or soon to join him hoped to build a Gnesio-Lutheran Wittenberg, but Wittenberg was in their very midst and was not as keen about their plans. Once again, students of Melanchthon, men sometimes too indomitable and smart for their own good, turned on each other with all the vigor and skill he had ingrained in them in the classroom.

Negotiations for Flacius' appointment had begun between him and Johann Friedrich I already in 1554, before the ruler died in March.[2] His sons resumed negotiations in 1555, but the process was delayed, in part because of Flacius' focus on the *Centuries*, which he was working tirelessly to bring to fruition. Negotiations at first focused especially on a role within the church. Since Flacius was never ordained, he could not serve as a pastor or chaplain. The princes wanted to find some way in which to appoint him to a supervisory position in the churches of their lands, as well as an advisory role to the court. Flacius' professorship was a late development but helped facilitate these goals.

The princes' desire to land Flacius within their realm is clear from their willingness to open their wallets. They offered an extremely generous salary to attract Flacius (300 imperial thalers annually), which stoked jealousy among his soon-to-be colleagues.[3] Amsdorf mediated negotiations and suggested that Flacius serve as general superintendent and professor. He, like the princes, seems to have

---

1 Olson, *Matthias Flacius and the Survival of Luther's Reform*, 328.

2 For more on Flacius' call to Jena and professorship there, see Daniel Gehrt, "Matthias Flacius as Professor of Theology in Jena and His Educational Enterprise in Regensburg," in *Matthias Flacius Illyricus*, ed. Irene Dingel, Johannes Hund, and Luka Ilić (Göttingen: Vandenhoeck & Ruprecht, 2019), 35–65.

3 Gehrt, "Matthias Flacius as Professor in Jena," 38.

been eager to bring Flacius to ducal Saxony. This shows that Amsdorf still thought highly of his Magdeburg comrade, even in the midst of their disagreement over the Eisenach Synod. Daniel Gehrt notes that Amsdorf probably hoped from the beginning that Flacius' acceptance of the position would help limit the influence of Viktorin Strigel at the university and in the court.[4]

Professor Flacius

When Flacius began teaching, he first lectured on Romans, which shaped the rest of his teaching of Paul's epistles and the New Testament as a whole. He also lectured at Jena on the Gospel of John, 1 and 2 Corinthians, and Galatians, and he taught Hebrew. He planned eventually to work his way through all of Paul's epistles in his lectures. As a professor, he lamented what he considered the excessive use of commentaries and urged active and substantive exegetical engagement with the texts of Scripture themselves. Was he a popular professor? It appears that attendance at his lectures was unimpressive. Amsdorf noted that he was not as gifted a teacher as his Gnesio-Lutheran colleagues Simon Musäus and Johann Wigand. Amsdorf, who had promoted Flacius for the position, would have had little reason to disparage Flacius' pedagogical abilities. Flacius himself provided explanations for the low numbers: students' desire to attend easier lectures based on the *loci* method rather than such an exegetical approach and the efforts of fellow faculty members to discourage attendance at his lectures, among other reasons.[5] Nonetheless, Flacius' reputation and especially his network of associates brought an eventual bump in enrollment at Jena as friends encouraged young men to attend and students were drawn from more distant lands because of his connections outside of Germany, especially in Austria.

Johann Stigel was the founding rector at Jena. Viktorin Strigel held the post next. Erhard Schnepff followed him. These three men formed a leadership core at the young academy. They were close friends. They were not happy with the prospect of Flacius serving with them.

4 Gehrt, "Matthias Flacius as Professor in Jena," 39.

5 Gehrt, "Matthias Flacius as Professor in Jena," 46.

They were less happy when it became a certainty. They resented the Illyrian's doctrinal intractability and his attacks on Melanchthon. That Flacius immediately stepped into such an influential role in the churches of ducal Saxony and with the court only upset them more. He was not merely a colleague at the academy. He would be exercising oversight over doctrine and practice in the duke's lands, lands in which they served. Moreover, Flacius' salary was significantly higher than theirs, even after their years of service. Flacius thus encountered immediate hostility that did not let up.

The Synergistic Controversy

As Flacius began his new life in Jena, another debate broke out between students of Melanchthon, this one about the role of the will in conversion: the Synergistic Controversy. "Synergism" refers to the will working with God in conversion, at least to some degree. Unsurprisingly, Flacius jumped into the dispute in print. Because he had been charged with oversight in the churches of ducal Saxony, it makes sense that he would be concerned about this doctrinal development in Leipzig, so close and so influential a town; but as in other theological controversies, Flacius again played an outsized role. This did not endear him to his already combative new colleagues who harbored Wittenberg sympathies.

When Erasmus wrote against Luther, he not only critiqued Luther's position on the bound will (that we do not have a free will in matters of salvation) but also complained that Luther made too much of original sin. It makes sense, therefore, that the controversy Flacius now joined over the human will and its role in salvation would later play into the debate over original sin, which would precipitate his downfall. In efforts to introduce the human will into conversion, Flacius and Amsdorf both saw a threat to Luther's whole theology and the entire enterprise of the Reformation, which they and their comrades in Magdeburg had worked so hard, at great personal risk, to preserve. When Erasmus attacked Luther's position on the will, Luther congratulated the humanist for going for his jugular, for attacking the core of his theology. Now Flacius saw a new enemy thrusting for the neck of Gospel proclamation.

For the Magdeburgers, the debate over free will was simply an extension of previous attacks on the Gospel. Indeed, like so many of the other disputes, it arose out of a desire to defend the Leipzig Interim and the spirit of theology that went into it. By this point, Amsdorf had been worried for decades about Melanchthon's changes to his *Loci*. Moreover, in the preface of a work translated by Caspar Cruciger, without naming Luther, Melanchthon had warned about "Stoic ravings about necessity and fate," and later he assailed the "fatalism" of those who focused too much on election.[6] Amsdorf, therefore, had matters of the will on his radar when it came to Melanchthon and his students.

Melanchthon had never been fond of Luther's great treatise on the bound will and had warned students about it. He thought it risked undermining human responsibility and turning people into nothing but blocks of wood in conversion. To be fair to Melanchthon, this was not the only time he thought Luther pushed too far in his writings. However, he never publicly accused Luther of error during their time together. Rather, here again we see a growing difference of emphasis between the two towering figures of the Wittenberg Reformation, one that boiled over among Melanchthon's students after Luther's death.

One of Melanchthon's students, Johann Pfeffinger, started the dispute about free will. He thought he was defending Melanchthon's teaching but, as with Georg Major, what he set forth was his take on the preceptor's position more than the preceptor's own. Making matters worse in the eyes of the Gnesio-Lutherans, Pfeffinger was a friend and supporter of Duke Moritz, who they still considered a traitor to Luther's teaching and the usurper of Johann Friedrich in electoral Saxony.[7] In this regard, Flacius had already written against Pfeffinger in 1551.[8] Again, almost everyone involved came at things through the lens of the interim crises. This was no abstract debate bereft of baggage. The matter was highly charged; the participants came with powder in their kegs.

The source of the conflict was a standard part of university life and education. Pfeffinger wrote theses about the will and conversion

---

6 Robert Kolb, *Bound Choice, Election, and Wittenberg Theological Method* (Grand Rapids: Eerdmans, 2005), 107.

7 Arand, Kolb, and Nestingen, *The Lutheran Confessions*, 201.

8 Flacius, *Gründliche verlegung aller Sophisterey*.

for debate at the University of Leipzig in 1555. Flacius and others quickly caught wind. When Amsdorf pounced, Flacius quickly followed. The only way the will was active in conversion, they argued, was in opposing it. Other Gnesio-Lutherans echoed the concerns of Amsdorf and Flacius. Melanchthon kept his distance as much as possible but did defend his teaching as expressed in his own writings. Now, however, he did accuse Luther of error. He said "that Luther had erred in the same direction as Gallus."[9] The Gnesio-Lutherans, in his view, were running with Luther's hyperbolic language and falling into the madness of the Stoics and their determinism. This was significant, especially decades after Luther's defining statements on the will.

Johann Pfeffinger's 1555 defense of the language of the Leipzig Interim in his *Propositions on the Free Will* flowed directly from the Adiaphoristic Controversy.[10] A dispute about practice revealed deep differences in theological emphases and even doctrine itself. While Pfeffinger's teaching was not Melanchthon's, it was not far from it. The preceptor had spoken of three causes in conversion already in his revised *Loci* of 1543. These causes were the Spirit, the voice of God, and the human will. The Spirit moved the heart. The voice of God called the sinner. The human will assented to that call.

Here it should be noted that questions about the human will and the degree to which the fall has wounded, or paralyzed, it are not idle. What a theologian holds about these things determines what he or she thinks about human beings, God, and the relationship between the two, especially how human beings are saved or obtain salvation. Justification was not one teaching among others for Flacius and the Gnesio-Lutherans. It was the hub of the wheel, the teaching from which all the others emerged like spokes, forming one complete, indivisible wheel. Doctrine was a unity, a totality, for them. Rather than "doctrines," they could speak just as often, or more often, about "doctrine," singular. Justification, moreover, was not simply a teaching. Justification was the work of Christ. It is what He came from heaven to earth to do. Christ was the sinner's justification. He was the sun, and doctrine and practice emanated from Him like rays. An assault on

9 Arand, Kolb, and Nestingen, *The Lutheran Confessions*, 204.

10 Irene Dingel, "The Culture of Conflict in the Controversies Leading to the Formula of Concord (1548–1560)," in *Lutheran Ecclesiastical Culture, 1550–1675*, ed. Robert Kolb (Leiden: Brill, 2008), 47.

doctrine and practice, then, was not an isolated thing. It was an attack on Christ and His work, justification. There was no God other than the one who justifies sinners in Christ, and there was no way to know this God other than through Christ, who justified sinners—sinners dead in sin, sinners with a will bound in sin, sinners who needed not a helping hand or nudge in the right direction but new life, and that as a gift. While the students of Melanchthon feared a loss of human responsibility through the removal of the assenting human will from conversion, that God would be nothing more than a puppet master, their opponents saw an attack on God Himself and the robbery of comfort and certainty from the believer.

Pursuing Unity and Orthodoxy

Even as this debate simmered, it had been decided at the Diet of Regensburg to continue dialogue between Roman Catholic and Evangelical theologians. A natural venue presented itself: the imperial Colloquy of Worms in late summer 1557. A ragtag assembly of Lutherans would take part, representing the fractured state of Lutheranism in Germany, as various territories sent delegations. Mirković explains that Flacius was not among this number because "he was fundamentally opposed to any attempt at reconciliation with Rome and, in addition, saw only a further weakening of evangelical unity and a sharper division in Lutheranism arising from talks between evangelicals and followers of Rome."[11] Flacius was thus tasked with helping to shape the approach the delegates from Ernestine Saxony would take, putting advisory thoughts on paper. These included a demand that those who had compromised during the Adiaphoristic Controversy be named. Flacius recognized that the Lutherans came into such talks divided. He was skeptical of what could be accomplished with such an array of voices in such a setting. If the Lutherans could not agree among themselves, what use would talks with Roman Catholics be at this point? It would only provide apologetic fodder

11 Mirković, *Matija Vlačić Ilirik*, 508.

for their opponents. While few probably expected any breakthroughs with Rome, there were hopes that increased unity could be fostered among Lutherans through the colloquy. Such hopes may have been naïve in Flacius' opinion, but some of the other theologians consulted by the princes shared such aspirations for improved relations within Lutheranism, and the court seemed inclined toward their optimism and openness. Such optimism proved fruitless, however. After an abundance of squabbling between Gnesio-Lutherans and Philippists in Worms, the delegation from Weimar, along with some others, walked out.[12] The Lutherans had put on quite the show for their Roman Catholic counterparts.

On February 25, 1558, in Frankfurt, Charles V transferred his imperial title to his brother, Ferdinand. This event drew a number of Lutheran princes. The desire for Evangelical unity still stood at the forefront of the concerns many brought. Discussions there led to the crafting of the Frankfurt Agreement, or Recess, a document that Melanchthon, who was also in Frankfurt, played a role in producing. This agreement drew the support of Elector Otto Henry of the Palatinate, Elector Augustus I of Saxony, Elector Joachim II of Brandenburg, Count Palatine Wolfgang of Zweibrücken, Duke Christopher of Württemberg, and Philip of Hesse, all of whom signed it on March 18, 1558. The rulers insisted that no further discussion of the disputed topics treated in the agreement would be tolerated. The matters were to be considered settled. Obviously, Flacius, Amsdorf, and other Gnesio-Lutherans opposed the agreement, especially with the threat of censorship of debate about issues that had been disputed for some time now: justification (Osiander), good works (Major), adiaphora, and the presence of Christ in the Lord's Supper. Ducal Saxony led the opposition, which other territories joined. They insisted that the agreement downplayed significant doctrinal differences and failed to address critical distinctions. This fueled a desire among some to have a more definitive statement on Lutheran doctrine for Ernestine Saxony.

Flacius picked up his campaign to maintain religious orthodoxy in the duke's territories. In a letter to the duke dated January 17, 1558, when lectures were being held but the privileges granted to the university had not yet been proclaimed, Flacius urged the prince to make

---

12 Ilić, *Theologian of Sin and Grace*, 141.

use of this occasion to ensure the doctrinal integrity of the school and his lands. Frustrated by the antagonism of his colleagues and the failure of the court to heed sufficiently his counsel regarding Worms, Flacius pushed for the duke to use the proclamation of the new university's privileges to state clearly and publicly and with his own voice the purpose of the school, namely, "the protection and defense of the divine legacy of Christ, Paul, and Luther."[13] Even more, Flacius advised the duke to explicitly name those false teachings that would not be tolerated, especially recent and current ones. No one should doubt where the duke and his churches stood on doctrine and practice. This, Flacius insisted, was necessary to preserve the vitality of the churches and schools of Thuringia.

The duke did not think the celebration an appropriate moment for such a statement. He wanted proper doctrine and practice, but he also wanted unity, and he did not agree with Flacius that such a proclamation would serve for unity. Rather, he thought it would exacerbate things and work against steps toward concord. The duke, however, did agree to outline what was and was not acceptable doctrine in the churches and schools of his land. To this end, he appointed a committee of three men: Schnepff, Strigel, and Andreas Hügel, a Jena superintendent. Flacius was not on the committee. The committee turned in its document April 3, 1558, and a meeting was scheduled for discussion of the draft. The church workers of ducal Saxony were invited to participate.

The meeting did not go well. Flacius condemned the document as insufficient. It had glossed over pivotal controversies from recent history. It failed to speak clearly against the errors of those who compromised during the Adiaphoristic Controversy. Things became heated. All the tension that had been building since Flacius' arrival, and even before, now spilled over. Each side saw confirmation of what it had suspected of the other. The duke was flummoxed. The point of the document was unity, but all it had accomplished was the threat of physical altercations among church workers and intense polemics between colleagues.

---

13 Mirković, *Matija Vlačić Ilirik*, 169–70.

The Weimar Book of Confutation

Johann Friedrich II decided to try again and appointed a new committee. The committee was not tasked with writing a new document but with building on the draft already in hand. The committee members were Maximilian Mörlin, Johann Stössel, and Simon Musäus, who met in Coburg and then Weimar. They handed in the product of their labors on November 25, and the duke added his concluding remarks on November 28, 1558. This version included a statement about the purpose of the university, which it noted had been founded by Johann Friedrich I, who had suffered for his faith as a captive after the defeat of the Schmalkaldic League and refused to accept theological compromises that might have improved his fortunes. Flacius' concerns had been addressed. The Gnesio-Lutherans had largely gotten what they wanted, and it bore the force of law. With this document, orthodoxy could be enforced by those overseeing the churches and schools.

There were nine articles in the Weimar *Book of Confutation*. The majority (six) dealt with teachings or groups all Lutheran parties condemned, such as Schwenkfeldians, Anabaptists, and those who denied the Trinity. The remaining three, however, aimed squarely at the Philippists. These dealt with the human will, good works, and adiaphora. Kolb notes that especially the *Book of Confutation* "demonstrate[s] that Flacius' influence at court—presumably strengthened by Amsdorf's support—was not only rising but was already unrivaled. The final text of the *Book of Confutation* reflected his views."[14] Flacius had triumphed. He, together with Amsdorf, had assembled a Gnesio-Lutheran contingent in Jena, reshaping the faculty and ministerium of ducal Saxony. He had undermined efforts at rapprochement with other Lutheran parties, unless they were undertaken with a clear expectation of a confession of guilt from those who had compromised under political pressure. He had persuaded the duke to bring the *Book of Confutation* into existence. Now he hoped to make sure that it was enforced.

Objections arose quickly from Strigel and others. Strigel protested the document's teaching about free will, its definition of the Gospel, its treatment of Major (who, he noted, had retracted his infamous

14 Kolb, *Nikolaus von Amsdorf*, 148.

formula about good works), and he accused it of generally misrepresenting the positions of Wittenbergers. Strigel would pay for his opposition before triumphing in his contest with Flacius.

Kolb points out that Duke Johann Friedrich II, a "respectable lay theologian who could read the Scriptures in their original languages," was most concerned with strengthening control over his lands and churches.[15] The fact that his theologians were more interested in fighting among themselves was a problem. It was Strigel's turn to annoy him now. It would be Flacius' later. After consulting Amsdorf and others, the duke faced a tough decision. If he wanted peace, it seemed he had to discipline Strigel, along with Hügel, who also rejected the *Book of Confutation*, the final form of the work they had started. On Holy Saturday 1559, troops broke down Strigel's door, seized him from his bed, and arrested him. He was joined by Hügel. Held in a fortress, attempts were made to win them over so that they would subscribe to the *Book of Confutation*. They refused to cave. Finally, because their imprisonment was causing diplomatic waves, they were released. Strigel spent nearly four more years under house and city arrest, however. The duke was no longer playing games with his theologians. His patience had run out.

The Weimar Disputation

Something had to be done to restore unity or, rather, to create a unity that had never really existed. Various suggestions were made. Strigel called for a theological synod at which differences could be worked out. Flacius opposed that idea. He suggested instead a disputation, a public disputation, between the two biggest personalities involved, he and Strigel. Strigel agreed to take part. The duke agreed to the plan. Flacius worked on theses with several others. The theses hit on all the big points of dispute. Included among them was the question of academic freedom, based on Strigel's insistence that he had the academic right to use Aristotelian terminology in his theological work.[16] The disputation began in Weimar on August 2, 1560. It

15 Kolb, *Nikolaus von Amsdorf*, 148.

16 For the points of dispute, see Matthias Flacius Illyricus, *Dispvtatio de originali peccato, et libero arbitrio contra praesentes errores* (Jena, 1559). For a thorough recounting of the debate, see Matthias Flacius, Victorinus Strigel, and Simon

was halted after the death of Johann Friedrich II's son, an infant. What was meant to be a pause turned into a full stop. The debate never picked up again. Nevertheless, its repercussions endured for the lifetimes of both men involved. For that reason, the disputation and the positions both men took in it deserve attention here.

The disputation centered on the question of conversion and the role in it of the human will. Specifically, did the will play an active role, even if to a very limited degree? Flacius, Gallus, Amsdorf, and Luther considered conversion new creation. Something dead was made alive. There was new birth. There was an emphasis on a break. Strigel did not come at conversion in this way. He stressed continuity instead of a break. Something within the sinner was reactivated, something that had been hibernating, hidden. When God hit the switch, this potentiality within the fallen sinner was activated. Strigel "believed this made it possible to speak of responsible decision-making by the individual."[17] Flacius and Amsdorf had suspected Strigel of unorthodoxy for a while. Now they were sure of his heterodoxy. He was a Philippist like so many others who had opposed the true religion of Christ, which they had worked tirelessly to protect. Providing even more vindication of their position, Strigel's later teaching on the Lord's Supper adopted a Reformed position, moving in a similar direction as some other Philippists as he aged.

Here perhaps some defense of Flacius' approach to this controversy is appropriate. Flacius had been tasked with the oversight of doctrine and practice. Even more, rather than shutting down discussion

---

Musäus, eds., *Disputatio de originali peccato et libero arbitrio inter Matthiam Flacium Illyricum & Victorinum Strigelium publice Vinariae per integram hebdomadam, praesentibus Illustriss. Saxonie Principibus, Anno 1560 initio mensis Augusti contra papistarum & synergistarum corruptelas habita cum praefatione, in qua & Disputationis huius utilitas, & editionis causae exponuntur. Cui succedunt Rationes, cur necessaria sit cognitio doctrinae & Disputationis de Libero arbitrio: & Discrimina verae ac falsae sententia. Accesserunt eiusdem argumenti et alia quaedam diversorum scripta eiusdem Disputationis occasione, ac illustrandae veritatis gratia composita: quorum alia quidem antea quoq; edita fuere, alia vero nunc primum in lucem prodeunt: Omnia triplo, quam antea edebantur, nunc auctiora, lectuq; dignissima, & nostro praefertim seculo ad formandum rectius de praefentibus controuersiis iudicium ultissima cognitu* (Basel: Johannes Oporinus, 1563).

17 Dingel, "Culture of Conflict," 50.

of the topic, he encouraged open debate. He believed the truth could be known, and would be shown, through public disputation. Diarmaid MacCulloch dismisses Flacius as "chief among these watchful, angry souls" who struggled against the compromises of Wittenberg, and elsewhere he speaks of the Gnesio-Lutherans as "ayatollahs."[18] While Flacius and the Gnesio-Lutherans certainly were not without fault in how they conducted themselves in various polemical battles, their conception of truth was the primary driver behind their readiness for debate and insistence upon agreement, not some lust for dissension or a tyrannical spirit. No doubt their personalities came into play, and no doubt their experiences colored how they interpreted things, but they sought to defend more than themselves, their careers, and their reputations. They saw the Gospel at stake, along with everything for which Luther had risked his life. Flacius would not have accepted the duke's invitation to a debate with Strigel if he wanted simply to censor his colleague. He could have worked in other ways toward that end. The duke wanted his theologians to be reconciled, and reconciliation was the goal of the debate that became known as the Weimar Disputation. That Flacius failed to accomplish this, and that he fell into error of his own, does not negate this.

The Weimar Disputation, which ran from August 2–8, was attended by the dukes and their advisers, church officials, and students from the university, as well as from the universities in Leipzig and Wittenberg. It took place three months after Melanchthon's death (April 19, 1560). Strigel set a trap from which Flacius could not—or would not—extricate himself. Finally, one of Melanchthon's disciples had managed what no one had before. Wittenberg at long last had its revenge. The Gnesio-Lutherans were divided as a result, and Flacius would never recover, although the Formula of Concord would adopt a position that recognized what led him to adopt the position and guarded against the errors of which he accused Strigel.

---

18 Diarmaid MacCulloch, *The Reformation: A History* (New York: Penguin, 2005), 349; Diarmaid MacCulloch, *The Boy King: Edward VI and the Protestant Reformation* (Berkeley: University of California Press, 2002), 170.

The Flacian Controversy

The Flacian Controversy—which the Formula of Concord opened with in Article I, followed by Article II, which tackled free will—owes its existence to the Weimar Disputation. The disputation was intended to address free will, but as with Erasmus, so with Strigel: one cannot assert any degree of a free will in matters of salvation without addressing the problem of original sin and its consequences for fallen human beings. Dingel explains: "The question of the free human will leads directly to the topic of original sin. Comments on the free will and its capabilities presupposed a definition of original sin and its implications for the human condition."[19] Flacius seemed to have sincerely believed he and Strigel would be able to come to agreement, but the disputation became the gateway to his own professional demise.[20] Flacius likely could have weathered the storm had he admitted his incautious use of language and further explained his position, but he refused to do so. Presumably, he thought that admitting his unwise use of language would strengthen Strigel's position. How much did pride play into things? That we cannot assess across centuries and without a view into his heart and mind. For whatever reasons, Flacius chose the route he did and bore the consequences, although not without protestations and attempts at a comeback.

Aristotelian terminology came to be the decisive issue of the debate. Flacius was insistent that the language of the Scriptures themselves should take precedence in theology and that, unless there was good reason for using them, Aristotelian concepts would only confuse things. He was not rejecting the use of philosophy entirely, or the use of Aristotelian language entirely, but he did think its unnecessary employment harmed the biblical truth in these central teachings of the Bible. Later, in his groundbreaking hermeneutical text, *Clavis Scripturae Sacrae*, or *Key to the Sacred Scriptures*, he would emphasize the need for biblical texts and their terminology to serve as the guide for the theological task.[21]

---

19 Dingel, "Culture of Conflict," 51.

20 Dingel, "Culture of Conflict," 51.

21 Arand, Kolb, and Nestingen, *The Lutheran Confessions*, 206.

What was the key Aristotelian sticking point? Strigel wanted to distinguish between the substance and accidents of human nature. He argued that original sin was not essential to human nature. According to Aristotle, a substance is something essential to a thing being what it is. If a thing loses it, it is no longer that thing. Strigel was not wrong in holding that original sin is not a substance of human beings as a whole. Adam and Eve were not created with original sin. Christ did not have original sin. However, Flacius and Strigel were not debating the nature of humans before the fall into sin or the human nature of the God-man. They were discussing the human nature of fallen sinners. Thus by holding that original sin was an accident, like chalk on a shirt or the length of fingernails, Strigel downplayed the consequences of the fall and the severity of the doctrine of original sin. Dingel breaks down the problem presented by both men's arguments: "Strigel correctly identified this distinction as widely-used; he was wrong in thinking it could help understand the biblical teaching on original sin and the free will. Flacius recognized correctly why that would not work, but he nonetheless decided to use this terminology which could only set the question in a false framework."[22] Flacius should have refused to debate on Strigel's terms, in this case, Aristotelian terms. He did not, however. He doubled down, which is what Strigel had hoped he would do. Strigel knew where he wanted the debate to go, and he knew his opponent well, and so he exploited his weakness.

Bente details how things unfolded:

> Strigel [plied Flacius] with the question: "*An negas peccatum originis esse accidens?* Do you deny that original sin is an accident?" Flacius answered: "*Lutherus diserte negat esse accidens.* Luther expressly denies that it is an accident." Strigel: "*Visne negare peccatum esse accidens?* Do you mean to deny that sin is an accident?" Flacius: "*Quod sit substantia, dixi Scripturam et Lutherum affirmare.* I have said that Scripture and Luther affirm that it is a substance."[23]

Thus Flacius did exactly what he was criticizing in his opponent: "joining biblical concepts and Aristotelian categories; he tried to express the biblical understanding of sin within this alien paradigm."[24]

22 Dingel, "Culture of Conflict," 52.

23 Bente, *Historical Introductions to the Lutheran Confessions*, 337.

24 Arand, Kolb, and Nestingen, *The Lutheran Confessions*, 206.

His colleagues and friends, both in ducal Saxony and elsewhere, would plead with Flacius for the rest of his life to acknowledge that his statements played into the accusations of Manichaeanism leveled against Luther's teaching of the bound will since the start of the Reformation. While Luther had spoken hyperbolically, Flacius had not. He meant what he said, if Aristotelian terms must be used. He took the imagery of Luther and the Bible and made a systematic point of it. He again and again insisted he was only speaking like the Bible, which spoke of sin as "flesh," of the "stony heart" of men, etc.[25]

Flacius made important distinctions in his teaching on original sin, but this was too late or was lost on many. Key to his understanding was a distinction between *substantia materialis* and *substantia formalis*, material substance and formal substance.[26] The material substance was intact still after the fall into sin. The formal, however, was lost. The material was neither good nor evil; it was indifferent. The formal had two parts, though. The higher part, *substantia formalis in summo gradu*, was where free will resided. The higher part gave human beings their real character before the fall, and Flacius saw this as the standard according to which theology was to consider what was essential to a human being.[27] This higher part was now lost, and worse than lost; it had been "turned into its evil opposite" by which people are now controlled. This meant that, "technically speaking, not all of human nature was substantially originally sin, but those components that were not had been so completely subjugated to the thralldom of original sin that the distinction was now moot."[28]

Flacius' view of man seems depressing and dismal, but it was not intended to be. Flacius did not think humanity had no dignity or goodness. People were still creatures of God, after all, men and women for whom Christ died. Flacius' emphasis on the utter sinfulness of human

---

25 Bente, *Historical Introductions to the Lutheran Confessions*, 337.

26 See Matthias Flacius Illyricus, *Altera Pars Clavis Scriptvrae, seu de Sermone Sacrarum literarum, plurimas generales Regulas continens: Avthore Matthia Flacio Albonense* (Basel: Paulus, 1567), 479–98.

27 Robert J. Christman, "'*Wir sindt nichts den eytel sunde*': The Impact of Flacius' Theology of Original Sin on the German Territory of Mansfeld," in *Matija Vlačić Illirik [III]* (Labin: Grad Labin, 2012), 109.

28 Christman, "*Wir sindt nichts den eytel sunde*," 110.

beings was a response drawn in opposition to Strigel's position that "in fallen sinners the power to do the good and moral remained."[29]

Bente, who admired Flacius and helped foster in generations of confessional American Lutherans an admiration of the Illyrian's zeal for pure doctrine, is nonetheless frank about Flacius' error: "The palpable mistake of Flacius was that he took the substantial terms on which he based his theory in their original and proper sense, while the Bible and Luther employ them in a figurative meaning, as the Formula of Concord carefully explains in its first article, which decided and settled this controversy."[30] Luther had said in his Genesis lectures that the essential characteristics of the human person as a whole no longer bore the image of God after the fall into sin.[31] He had also used the metaphor of a block of stone or wood regarding the sinner in conversion. Strigel played on this. He called Luther's talk about the will in *Bondage of the Will* a "horrid way of speaking" and thus played on Flacius' almost irresistible sense of responsibility to defend the great reformer and perhaps his greatest work.[32] Bente writes: "In making his statement concerning the substantiality of original sin, the purpose of Flacius was to wipe out the last vestige of spiritual powers ascribed to natural man by Strigel, and to emphasize the doctrine of total corruption, which Strigel denied. His fatal blunder was that he did so in terms which were universally regarded as savoring of Manicheism."[33]

Flacius refused to budge. He staked his career and his family's stability on the stance he had taken and he, along with them, endured innumerable trials because of it. He thought too much was at stake to concede even an inch. According to Christman, "Flacius' goal was to demonstrate unequivocally that humankind in no way contributed to its own salvation."[34] Salvation was at stake.

It is worthwhile to note that Flacius' anthropology—his view of the fallen sinner as lost, dead, and without any free will in matters of salvation—did not lead, as his opponents accused, to antinomianism.

29 Dingel, "Culture of Conflict," 52.

30 Bente, *Historical Introductions to the Lutheran Confessions*, 337.

31 Dingel, "Culture of Conflict," 52.

32 Kolb, *Bound Choice*, 160–61.

33 Bente, *Historical Introductions to the Lutheran Confessions*, 337.

34 Christman, "*Wir sindt nichts den eytel sunde*," 110.

He and those who held his view did not consider human beings as incapable of virtue in civic righteousness or the righteousness of the philosophers. People could do good things. They just could not do good things that availed as righteousness before God. They could not produce divine righteousness, which came only as a gift. Even more, the reality of new obedience played a prominent role in their theology. The believer would do new things as a new creation. Robert Kolb aptly dismisses allegations of antinomianism among the Gnesio-Lutherans because of their teachings on the bound will. They did not deny "the integrity of the human creature." They affirmed that God had created human beings "to function responsibly according to his divine definition of what it means to be human."[35] Kolb uses as an example Nikolaus Gallus, the Magdeburg comrade who remained a friend of Flacius even after the Weimar Disputation and who coauthored with Flacius more than one work on Luther's teaching regarding good works and the human will. Kolb notes that "on the basis of *De servo arbitrio*, Nikolaus Gallus rejected the idea that the free will apart from God's aid has any power to repent and practice the Christian life, even as he acknowledged the necessity of this life of repentance and obedience." That did not mean that Gallus was unconcerned with repentance and obedience, however. Rather, Gallus and his theological allies "sought to cultivate a life of love, that is, true human freedom, by binding their hearers once again to God's promises in Christ."[36]

Repercussions

Flacius' situation in Jena deteriorated as he and some of his allies overplayed their hands. Not long before the Weimar Disputation, on July 8, 1560, Matthias Wesenbeck, a Jena jurist, was asked to serve as a godfather at the Baptism of a poetry professor at the university, Johann Stigel. Superintendent Balthasar Winter, who was a Flacian, insisted that Wesenbeck could only do so after stating his agreement with the *Book of Confutation*. Wesenbeck objected. He was a jurist. In his view, there was no reason for such a demand. Musäus and Wigand became involved, and Wesenbeck was excommunicated, a startling development, which was appealed to the court in Weimar. Winter

35 Kolb, *Bound Choice*, 165.

36 Kolb, *Bound Choice*, 166.

was supposed to keep a low profile during the appeal, but he did the opposite. He and other Flacians, again including Musäus and Wigand, openly preached against opposition to the *Book of Confutation* and held out the threat of more excommunications.[37]

In September, soon after the Weimar Disputation, Winter refused the Sacrament of the Altar to a law professor who claimed that theology could be learned from Seneca.[38] None of this sat well with the court or with a good number of students. Some Gnesio-Lutherans—Amsdorf among them—warned against these actions, recognizing the damage they were doing. Flacius, however, sided with his friends and complained to the duke, who he thought was overstepping his bounds by attempting to silence these church workers. This only made matters worse. The duke had heard enough and stepped in directly. Winter was dismissed from office in late October. Flacius and Strigel were summoned to Weimar in December.

Matters only grew more contentious. The duke was convinced he had lost control of his theologians who rejected his efforts to supervise their work more closely. In February 1561, Johann Stössel was appointed superintendent in Jena. On April 22, tired of Flacius' allies using the pulpit to gripe about their changing fortunes, the duke prohibited their preaching. Censorship increased. The duke established new consistory oversight on July 8, 1561, which he led. All church workers in Thuringia were to submit to the authority of the consistory. The "contempt and abuse of excommunication" was given as a main reason for the new law.[39] Flacius wanted to appeal beyond the consistory to a general synod. He thought the state was overstepping. This, too, did not go well. The makeup of the consistory was unfavorable for Flacius and his friends. Musäus, reading the writing on the wall, accepted a superintendency in Bremen. Matthaeus Judex, an ally, was ousted on October 1, 1561, for publishing a document abroad that asked "how someone should behave toward the Antichrist, the papacy."[40]

37 Preger, *Matthias Flacius Illyricus und seine Zeit*, 2:134–35.

38 Ilić, *Theologian of Sin and Grace*, 153.

39 Preger, *Matthias Flacius Illyricus und seine Zeit*, 2:158.

40 Preger, *Matthias Flacius Illyricus und seine Zeit*, 2:165.

This left Flacius and Wigand. Flacius' days seemed numbered, and they were. There was no longer any patience for objections about procedure or injustice. There was no longer any desire to hear theological squabbling. Only their deposition remained. Summoned to the castle in Jena, Flacius and Wigand were stripped of their offices in front of the faculty, church workers, and town council on December 10, 1561.[41] Flacius and his family were on the move again and would be for the rest of his life. Gehrt notes that Flacius still had career prospects, including the possibility of a position at the University of Rostock, an invitation to return to Magdeburg with Wigand and Judex, and an offer of asylum in Mansfeld.[42] All these opportunities pulled him north, but Flacius wanted to go south. He had aspirations. He wanted to make use of his network to help foster Evangelical theology in Austria and southeastern Europe. He was interested in starting schools. This was ambitious for a man who had just lost his dream job, but Flacius was confident. To make things work, though, he needed a friend. Nikolaus Gallus, superintendent in Regensburg, was that friend.

41 Preger, *Matthias Flacius Illyricus und seine Zeit*, 2:173.

42 Gehrt, "Matthias Flacius as Professor in Jena," 53.

REGENSBURG, CHURCH HISTORY, AND HERMENEUTICS

FLACIUS MADE HIS way along the icy path to his new home in Regensburg in January 1562, dreaming of schools, a printing press, and the spread of Evangelical theology southward, down toward his homeland. Toward this end, Flacius had designs on the Slavic printing press currently in Urach, established by Hans Ungnad. He hoped to move it to Regensburg as part of his plans to foster Slavic reformation from this new base.[1] His family followed Flacius to Regensburg in February "not entirely without means," having accumulated some wealth over the previous years.[2] He likely had eight children in tow. Yet not all of Flacius' family left Jena. His oldest son, also named Matthias, remained a student there.[3]

---

1 Ilić, *Theologian of Sin and Grace*, 165.

2 Preger, *Matthias Flacius Illyricus und seine Zeit*, 2:229.

3 Ilić, *Theologian of Sin and Grace*, 161.

Flacius' presence in Regensburg was not welcomed by everyone. He was not just any refugee. He came with a controversial reputation. Some city leaders worried about repercussions for harboring him. He was granted asylum, but on the condition that he keep a low profile. He could only teach in his home. He was forbidden from printing. Regensburg's leaders were not looking for trouble, and they wanted to make sure that Flacius was not either. They were motivated especially by complaints from prominent figures, including Duke Johann Friedrich II, who did not want Flacius and Nikolaus Gallus stoking up more troubles in his territories from afar. That Flacius was allowed to stay was a testimony to Gallus' persistence and the support of friends, including Amsdorf. Flacius settled in. He had no employment in the city and no formal function in the church. Nevertheless, he was determined to make the best of his new situation, focusing on the academy he hoped to found. The family would remain in Regensburg for five years. While many of his plans did not come to fruition, Flacius did find time to write.

While in Regensburg, Flacius paid careful attention to developments elsewhere and, as one might suspect, could not help but give his opinion. With the accession of Friedrich III as Elector Palatine in 1559 had come movement in that territory toward Calvinism. Before this, there had been a mix of Gnesio-Lutherans, Philippists, and Calvinists. As the new elector studied theology, and became frustrated by the religious division in his realm, he grew tired of the contentiousness of the Lutheran parties. He felt drawn to Reformed positions. In early 1561, Elector Palatine Friedrich publicly adopted Reformed theological doctrines. This led to the formulation of the Heidelberg Catechism, published in 1563. This confession eventually became one of the Three Forms of Unity, the preeminent Reformed confessions, together with the Belgic Confession and the Canons of Dort. That it came out of a territory that had once been decidedly Lutheran added insult to injury for the aggrieved Lutheran theologians of Germany. Flacius vigorously opposed the Heidelberg Catechism. He also closely followed the development of the Crypto-Calvinist Controversy in Nuremberg. He even visited the city in 1562, after which he and Gallus issued an open letter about the conflict. When another Crypto-Calvinist Controversy erupted in Danzig, in Prussia, Flacius offered his counsel again. While he was no longer as deeply in the mix of things, he made sure to keep his antenna up and play whatever limited roles he could in shaping German Lutheranism.[4]

Flacius traveled somewhat often during his time in Regensburg. He went to Frankfurt frequently. He went to Mainz, Basel, and Augsburg. In Augsburg, Flacius personally, with an audience, delivered to the emperor himself, Maximilian II, his *De translatione Imperii Romani ad Germanos,* dedicated to the emperor and the German princes.[5] While his stay in Regensburg was tenuous, Flacius was hardly an outlaw.

Misfortune struck Flacius' family during this time. Elizabeth died giving birth to their twelfth child in early 1564. She had been with him for eighteen years, through thick and thin. He was overcome with grief. He told Gallus: "Amid tears and worries I consume myself, and not an hour goes by without my departed companion's image appearing before my soul. I often think that with so many crosses she never advised me to do anything bad, even though she was not the strongest in body and mind as a result of the many births."[6] Elizabeth had supported him to the end, managing the household faithfully and almost exclusively, even when it only increased her hardships.

Flacius struggled to take care of himself and the eight surviving children.[7] His diet suffered. He fell ill, suffering from stomach issues. Nine months after Elizabeth's death, Flacius lost his oldest daughter. His friends were concerned. He seemed at his breaking point. His friends urged Flacius to find a new wife, which he did, marrying Magdalena Ilbeck, the daughter of a deceased pastor. They were married on October 23, 1564. They would have six children during their marriage.

4 For more on these controversies and Flacius' involvement, see Ilić, *Theologian of Sin and Grace*, 166–84.

5 Preger, *Matthias Flacius Illyricus und seine Zeit*, 2:281.

6 Preger, *Matthias Flacius Illyricus und seine Zeit*, 2:232.

7 There is lack of clarity regarding the death of Flacius' first wife, the exact number of children they had before arriving in Regensburg, and the number of children surviving after her death.

The Clavis Scripturae Sacrae

Flacius continued work on the *Magdeburg Centuries* while in Regensburg. The most significant product of this time, however, was his *Clavis Scripturae Sacrae*, perhaps his most important work of scholarship, which was largely completed during his Regensburg years. At Jena, Flacius had exhorted his students to go to the Scriptures, to the source, rather than leaning on commentaries. He had written all sorts of pamphlets in Magdeburg about the power of the Word and the need to stand under it and not above it, calling Christians to listen, to hear what God says to them in Scripture. The Scriptures had led him north to Germany, and he had thrown himself into them as a student and as a teacher. Now Flacius wrote a book about how to understand the Scriptures. This was his most systematic undertaking, and it was a massive work, ranging from principles of interpretation to doctrinal formulations to a dictionary of biblical terms.

Flacius did not use the term "hermeneutics" for his work in the *Clavis*. That word made its appearance almost a century later.[8] However, Flacius' work was hermeneutics—perhaps the first significant work of its kind. Luther had insisted that the Holy Scriptures interpret themselves. Critics claimed this was an impossibility. How could Scripture be authoritative if there were so many different interpretations? Flacius' motivating conviction was that Luther was right and that problems in interpretation rested in the interpreter, not in the biblical text. This doctrinal conviction led him to set forth the principles in the *Clavis* that he believed would enable readers to understand the Word rightly, on its terms. "Flacius wanted to consistently apply the Reformation principle of *sola scriptura* exegetically and hermeneutically."[9]

8 For more information on this and the *Clavis*, see Hans-Peter Grosshans, "Hermeneutik als Schlüssel zur Wahrheit: Die *Clavis Scripturae Sacrae* des Matthias Flacius Illyricus," in *Matthias Flacius Illyricus*, ed. Irene Dingel, Johannes Hund, and Luka Ilić (Göttingen: Vandenhoeck & Ruprecht, 2019), 175–89.

9 Grosshans, "Hermeneutik als Schlüssel," 187.

The *Clavis* had two parts, the first of which (*Clavis Scripturae Sacrae seu de Sermone Sacrarum Literarum in duas partes divisae*) contains an impressive theological dictionary.[10] Flacius provided the history behind terms as well as their use in the Scriptures and the church. The definition of "faith" went on for pages.[11] Flacius hit on all the points of emphasis one might expect. The same was true of "grace."[12] He noted that improper definitions of this word, which had a very specific meaning in the Scriptures when connected to justification, had led to many "most pernicious errors."[13] The word "adiaphora" received one page of attention too. Flacius explained that in the church an adiaphoron was something "neither approved nor disapproved in and of itself," that was "neither forbidden nor commanded by God." In normal times, this included things such as music, readings, vestments, and ceremonies. Christians should act as neither "brutes nor captives" in these common matters.[14]

To understand the Scriptures, readers needed to understand the words and concepts the biblical authors used. These words and concepts could be defined according to their context and by comparing their usage throughout the Bible (and with the help of the liberal arts). Biblical passages enlightened each other, so that the proper meaning came from the Scriptures themselves and not from church fathers or other interpreters or authorities. The only authority in this regard was the Word itself, divinely inspired. If this was true of the church fathers, who were helpful, although not authoritative, this was even more true of the philosophers. Flacius was clear that the Scriptures themselves should define terms and concepts, not Aristotle or other philosophers, Christian or not. The errors of scholasticism needed to be avoided.

---

10 Matthias Flacius Illyricus, *Clavis Scriptvrae S, seu de Sermone Sacrarum, Authore Matthias Flacio Illyrico. Pars Prima: in qua singvlarum vocvm atque locotionum S. Scripturae usus ac ratio Alphabetico ordine explicatur* (Basel: Johannes Oporinus & Eusebius Episcopius, 1567).

11 Flacius, *Clavis Scriptvrae . . . Pars Prima*, 408–31.

12 Flacius, *Clavis Scriptvrae . . . Pars Prima*, 489–99.

13 Flacius, *Clavis Scriptvrae . . . Pars Prima*, 489.

14 Flacius, *Clavis Scriptvrae . . . Pars Prima*, 29–30.

The second part of the *Clavis* dealt with principles or rules for dealing with the Scriptures.[15] Central to these rules was the conviction that Christ was their interpretive key and that they must be read with the distinction between Law and Gospel in mind. Flacius was entirely of the same mind as Luther in this regard. Law and Gospel must be rightly distinguished not only for pastoral care and for making correct theological judgments but also for proper textual interpretation.[16] Reason and knowledge of the language, history, and culture mattered. One could not fully understand the text without the use of these aids. Christ, Law and Gospel, and the Spirit's activity were also necessary for proper interpretation. One should know what the Bible is about when approaching it, how God relates to us in it, and why. Here God came to sinners and revealed Himself in Christ, who was made the sinner's own by the Spirit, who condemned the sinner through the Law and made the sinner alive through the Gospel, so that sinners became saints. Flacius made this plain in the second "remedy" for obstacles in understanding texts, the first remedy being God Himself, who makes Christians *theodidaktoi*, "taught by God": "The second remedy is specific instruction or indeed more fruitful knowledge of those things that are dealt with in Holy Scripture, provided by the pious and experienced servants of Christ. This certainly consists above all in an awareness of our sickness and subsequently also of the only physician, Christ."[17]

Flacius unfortunately used much of the sixth tract of the second part of the *Clavis* to focus on his teaching of original sin. He expanded upon distinctions he had already made in or after the Weimar Disputation. This would cause him even more trouble than had his statements at Weimar. Nevertheless, for anyone who wanted to comprehend what he taught regarding the doctrine, this was the place to look, and it still is for interested scholars today. That Flacius felt the need to include it and other controversies after Luther's death in this tract and in the *Clavis* in general shows how fundamentally he saw them tied to a proper understanding of Scripture. This helps explain

15 *Altera Pars Clavis Scriptvrae.*

16 Grosshans, "Hermeneutik als Schlüssel," 185.

17 Matthias Flacius, *How to Understand the Sacred Scriptures from the Clavis Scripturae Sacrae*, trans. Wade R. Johnston (Saginaw, MI: Magdeburg Press, 2011), 63.

why he was so unwilling to retract his language until the very end of his life.

Continuing Uncertainty

Flacius' Regensburg days were drawing to a close. He was soon expelled from the city primarily because of outside pressure. The emperor himself, Maximilian II, ordered his asylum canceled. Although Maximilian had been an early admirer of Flacius' work, financially supporting some of it, he soured with time because of the persistent complaining of Elector Augustus of Saxony. Flacius left Regensburg in 1566, but his family remained behind for the time being. Surely Magdalena must have wondered what she had gotten into, so soon left to take care of Flacius' family all by herself, uncertain of what the future might hold. Such was Flacius' life at this point, and he would be a man on the move for the rest of his days, which meant Magdalena and the children would be a family on the move as well. Sad as the Regensburg sojourn had been, and as unfruitful as his attempts were to start an academy or establish a printing press, he had nevertheless accomplished much. His pen had been busy. He had put into print big ideas.

Flacius transformed disciplines. In his own day, people recognized that nothing like his church history and hermeneutical work had been done before, at least not since antiquity. There were more than a few who used his works, though they dare not admit it. He had an original mind and an amazing gift for organization. He had an impressive network and an eye for manuscripts. He recognized lacunae in the Protestant theological scholarship and sought to fill them. Even amid instability and persecution, deserved or not, he produced groundbreaking works. From his prodigious output in Magdeburg, reshaping modern propaganda; to the *Catalog* and the *Centuries*, reshaping the historical discipline; to the *Clavis*, which helped give birth to modern scientific hermeneutics, even his harshest critics benefited from his contributions to these fields. Those who, across centuries, lament his doctrinal polemics still must admit his enormous contribution to modern scholarship.

Regensburg allowed Flacius a chance to recommit himself to his most important projects, the *Centuries* and the *Clavis*. After years of controversy, he returned to what he had been preparing for since Venice (although he never really stopped working on such things). When engaging especially with these texts, one wonders what a Flacius without the Adiaphoristic Controversy might have been. As gifted a polemicist as he was, his historical and hermeneutical work provides more insight into his brilliance than his other projects. Flacius and his friends gave Protestants the early advantage in academic theology in both these fields. Thus patristics, modern church history (and history in general), and modern biblical hermeneutics (and scientific hermeneutics in general) owe a good measure of their evolution to the Illyrian and the early generations of Lutherans who collaborated and built on his work.

A WANDERER'S LIFE

Final Attempts to Recover a Reputation; Flacius' Death

Flacius spent the rest of his life looking for a new home and revitalization of his career. This journey began as he made his way to Antwerp in October 1566, during the Wonderyear, a period of Protestant gains between the Easters of 1566 and 1567. The Reformed were especially aggressive during this time, but several German Lutherans had been invited to the city by their coreligionists to help organize the Evangelical churches. There was debate about which way things should go, since the Protestant minority, seeking to make the most of what would be a brief period of religious toleration, included both Lutheran and Reformed Christians. Some pushed for a union church. Flacius obviously opposed this notion.

While in Antwerp, Flacius worked on a confession for the Lutherans there, the Antwerp Confession, published in 1567. During his stay, the *Clavis* was published in Basel. Flacius left Antwerp in early spring for what he thought would be a short absence to meet his family in Frankfurt as they traveled to Antwerp, their new home. He was mistaken. While he was gone, things took a turn for the worse. On February 20, Margaret of Parma ordered that all Protestant (heretic) services cease. All pastors were commanded to leave the city. The army was sent in less than a month later. The Reformed offered some resistance, but the Lutherans refused to take up arms with them. The Spanish army arrived on April 26, and the duke of Alba was about to begin his brutal oppression. Many Lutherans and Reformed fled. Flacius' hopes that he had found a new home for his family were dashed.

Flacius received temporary permission to stay in Frankfurt while he found a new home. Magdalena gave birth to another son in May. When the town council decided his time to stay had run out, he set his eyes on Strasbourg, where he hoped to find a more amenable situation. He was granted asylum until the end of the summer, and then a regular process of applications for extensions began. Throughout Flacius' time in Strasbourg, powerful opponents pressured the city government to expel him, including Emperor Maximilian II and Elector Augustus I of Saxony. Flacius' opposition to the failed Altenburg Colloquy (October 1568 to March 1569), with its attempt to foster unity in ducal and electoral Saxony, had only agitated Augustus I even more.

There was a brief chance for reconciliation offered by Jakob Andreae. He had visited Flacius in Stuttgart just before the move to Strasbourg. Johann Brenz met with him as well. The idea was floated of a set of doctrinal articles upon which they and others might agree. Andreae put the articles together, without Flacius' participation and without his approval. Flacius objected to the articles on principle, there were no antitheses. Flacius had objected to such articles in the past. He thought any statement of accepted beliefs should include condemned positions. This was not received well. Andreae and other Lutherans saw this as more unnecessary divisiveness. Flacius lost yet another opportunity to reenter the Lutheran mainstream and reverse his fortunes.

A new debate over original sin broke open. While Flacius' statements about this doctrine in the Weimar Disputation had been known for some time, his publication of a defense of his view and expanded statements (in an attempt to clarify his position) in the *Clavis* brought disputes about this doctrine to the forefront. Those who had been silent before, or who had not considered his statements in the Weimar Disputation to be a serious issue given their context, now entered the fray, including some of his former friends and allies. As in the past, Flacius refused to back down. He only upped his defense. Gnesio-Lutheranism was further divided.

An opportunity for optimism nevertheless arose in ducal Saxony. Duke Johann Friedrich II, who had brought about Flacius' downfall in his territories, now met his own demise. Like his father, he found himself a captive of the emperor. His army had attacked Würzburg in a bid to regain lands he thought rightfully his. Feelers were also put out for aid in overthrowing Elector Augustus I of Saxony. Assassination seems to have been the preferred method. The imperial ban was placed upon Johann Friedrich II in 1566, and Augustus I marched on Gotha and captured Johann Friedrich without a fight. He remained an imperial prisoner until his death in 1595. Johann Wilhelm, the second son of Johann Friedrich I, succeeded his brother. This seemed a positive turn of events. Johann Wigand returned to Jena. The *Book of Confutation* regained authority. But while many Flacians benefited from the new duke's Gnesio-Lutheran sympathies, Matthias Flacius was not one of them. Inviting Flacius to Jena would have been a step too far, given Johann Wilhelm's tenuous position with the emperor and with his cousin in electoral Saxony. Moreover, not every Flacian was still a friend. Many were not all that keen on being considered "Flacians" any longer. While Nikolaus Gallus remained a faithful friend until his death in 1570, not everyone was willing to agree to disagree or to risk personal repercussions for standing by the nomadic polemicist with an unbecoming stubbornness regarding Aristotelian terms he had not even wanted to use in the first place.

The Glossa

While Flacius spent much of this time occupied with the debate over original sin, he continued his work on the New Testament. His enormous *Glossa* was published in Basel in 1570.[1] In hopes of winning

1 Matthias Flacius Illyricus, ΤΗΣ ΤΟΥ ΥΙΟΨ ΘΕΟΥ ΚΑΙΗΣ ΔΙΑΘΗΚΗΣ ΑΠΑΝΤΑ *Novvm Testamentum Jesu Christi Filii Dei, Ex Versione Erasmi, Innumeris in Locis ad Graecem veritatem, genuinumque sensum*

favor, he dedicated the book to the city council in Strasbourg at a time when he again needed permission to extend his stay.[2] This would be his last substantial publication. In this impressive book, Flacius ended where things had begun, with the Scriptures. This was also a return to his Venetian education, as he built upon and emended the work of the great humanist Erasmus, whose imprint he had personally experienced during his time in Basel, the city from which some of Flacius' most important works had been published over the years.

Flacius continued to publish regarding original sin. The more it cost him, the more he persisted. Strasbourg continued to face pressure for providing him asylum. This only became worse as Flacius continued to defend his position. The city was accused of harboring a heretic and thus supporting heresy. On August 10, 1571, Flacius met with Andreae again. They discussed original sin. Andreae again cautioned against Flacius' use of the Aristotelian term "substance." Flacius insisted the use of the term was appropriate in light of the distinctions he made. The meeting went better than expected, but nothing lasting came of it. Tensions heightened between Flacius and the city government and its clergy. Finally, Flacius was willing to compromise, at least a little. He suggested dropping the use of the term "substance" and instead speaking about "substantial powers."[3] Flacius' time in Strasbourg, however, was nearing its end.

The Mansfeld Colloquy

Even as his continuing presence in Strasbourg became increasingly contentious, Flacius made a surprising trip to Mansfeld, where he appeared at the castle unannounced. This, too, was connected to his

---

emendata. Glossa Compendiara M. Matthiae Flacij Illyrici Albonensis in nouum Testamentum. Cum multiplici indice tum ipsius sacri Textus, tum etiam glossae. Quid praeterea sit in commodum Lectoris in hac editione praestitum, sequens nuncupatoria praestatio indicabit (Basel, 1570).

2 Johannes Hund, "Kompromisslosigkeit, wachsende Isolation und Verfolgung: Das Exil des Flacius in Strassburg und seine letzten Jahre in Frankfurt am Main," in *Matthias Flacius Illyricus*, ed. Irene Dingel, Johannes Hund, and Luka Ilić (Göttingen: Vandenhoeck & Ruprecht, 2019), 88.

3 Preger, *Matthias Flacius Illyricus und seine Zeit*, 2:371.

teaching on original sin, which had come to dominate his life and work. One wonders what more he could have produced, building on the *Clavis*, the *Glossa*, and the *Centuries*, had he not been consumed with debates about this doctrine. There was no Flacius who was not this Flacius though, and he was convinced that concessions would undermine the Gospel and Luther's Reformation. He came to Mansfeld to defend himself against accusations regarding his teaching on original sin. As often happened, he argued that the allegations leveled against him ignored the distinction he made between the natural powers of fallen human beings and the human being as a whole. He was no Manichaean, he insisted. He had not turned the devil into a creator. Sin was not the substance of the human being without qualification. He had been maligned by Andreas Fabricius in a letter to the court, he asserted, and so deserved a hearing.

Flacius asked for a colloquy, and it was held September 3–4, 1572. The Eisleben pastors discussed his teaching and expressed their concerns about it and its implications. Fabricius argued that human nature differed from the Law only *in quantum*, insofar as it was corrupted. Flacius pointed out the key difference between them. He insisted that human nature differed from the Law not *in quantum* but *quia*, because it is corrupted.[4] The count issued a judgment in Flacius' favor, but Flacius had not won over those among the Eisleben clergy who objected to his teaching.

When Flacius arrived back in Strasbourg, the council made it clear that it was time for him to leave the city. He, Magdalena, and the children would have to find refuge elsewhere. In spring 1573, he set out to find a new home, however temporary. On his way, he debated the Jesuits of Fulda. Finally, he found a place where he and his family could stay. He returned to Strasbourg and gathered up his household, leaving on June 8, 1573. Their new home was in the former Cistercian monastery in Frankfurt-am-Main. He arrived there in poor health and tired of this world, an exhausted wanderer.

From his new home, Flacius visited Count Vollrad in Mansfeld; Elector Johann Georg in Berlin, along with Andreas Musculus, the general superintendent; and then Count Sebastian Zedlitz in Silesia, among others. In Silesia, Flacius attended a colloquy where he again discussed original sin. Feeling at ease because of the friendly flow of

---

4 Preger, *Matthias Flacius Illyricus und seine Zeit*, 2:375.

conversation, he was willing again to consider dropping use of the word "substance" so long as others would drop the term "accident." In Strasbourg, he had expressed such a disposition in the face of expulsion. Now he discussed the possibility without any such fear.[5] This was overall a pleasant trip for him. He returned to Frankfurt as the summer wound down. His health had declined more.

Final Years and Final Confession

Flacius' return was not met with happy news. Weary and ill, unable to establish a rhythm to life or provide stability for his family because of living at the mercy of others, Flacius again faced the threat of expulsion. Elector Augustus I continued his implacable campaign against him, a hostility stemming from the siege of Magdeburg, during which time Flacius and the Magdeburg theologians had condemned the activities of Moritz as treacherous, undermined his legitimacy in his new lands, and questioned the validity of his new electoral title. Wherever Flacius sought refuge, Augustus I worked to see it denied him or revoked, had it been granted.

This continued in Frankfurt. Katharina von Meerfeld, the prioress of a Lutheran convent for widows, orphans, and others in need, worked tirelessly to preserve this refuge for Flacius and his family. Pressures continued to mount, however. There was only so much the prioress and others could do, including Magdalena, Flacius' wife, who pled for mercy for her family and her ill husband. It is hard to imagine how the news of yet another expulsion must have hit him on the heels of the perhaps unanticipated warmth he had experienced during some of his recent stops. Surely the difficulty this would cause his wife and children disturbed him more than its impact upon himself. The mental strain must have only exacerbated his physical ailments.

During his last few years, Flacius wrote a catechism, perhaps for use by his own children. This was not intended to supplant Luther's but was to be used alongside it. He dedicated it to Katharina von

5 Preger, *Matthias Flacius Illyricus und seine Zeit*, 2:386–87.

Meerfeld, whom he called his "gracious mother."[6] He was grateful for the kindness she had shown his family. As one might suspect, the catechism dealt with Flacius' teaching on original sin.

Flacius had been working on a *Glossa* on the Old Testament at the end of his life, but he was unable to complete it, distracted by polemics with Andreae, stomach issues, and a lack of energy. He was ordered to leave Frankfurt-am-Main after May 1, when his last extension of asylum would run out. However, Flacius would wander no more; it was time to go home. On March 10, 1575, his son Daniel called for pastors to visit so Flacius could receive the Lord's Supper and give his final statement of faith, including his position on original sin and the Lord's Supper, about which debates had roared since the Crypto-Calvinist controversies. Flacius was in great pain, however. Hartmann Beyer and Matthias Ritter, the pastors who had come, promised to return the next day. Flacius told his wife and children when they left:

> My life is in the hand of God, who deals with me according to His gracious will and good pleasure. I might suffer, but I hope to be strong enough to do two things still: the spiritual, concerning my confession, to write it down at the end, and the secular, concerning you, how you should manage after my death. So far as the spiritual matter is concerned, however, I point to my various books and writings; whoever does not want to be informed about them and understand my opinion properly, that one will not be helped any more by a short confession.[7]

Regarding the secular concern, Flacius was able to leave a remarkable amount of wealth to his family. While his last years had been difficult and he had struggled to find employment, he had saved enough to provide for them after his passing.

His pain increased during the night. His doctor, Adam Lonicer, gave him a sleeping aid (laudanum, an opiate) to ease his suffering. Matthias Flacius Illyricus Albonensis died the next morning

6 Ilić, *Theologian of Sin and Grace*, 223. Matthias Flacius Illyricus, *Eine Einfeltige Christliche Vnterweisunge der gewachssenen Jugend in den noetigsten Stuecken des Christlichen Glaubens / so auff den kleinen Catechismum folgen solt / Sampt Anzeigung der jetzigen widerwertigen Jrthumen / auff das sie erkenne beide das Gute / zur erwehlung / vnd auch das Boese / zur vermeidung. M. Matthias Flacius Jllyricus. Anno 1577* (1577).

7 Preger, *Matthias Flacius Illyricus und seine Zeit*, 2:525–26.

at nine o'clock. The date was May 11, 1575. He was fifty-five years old. He closed his eyes and breathed his last in peace. The faith that had buoyed him through so many trials remained until the end. His doctor, Pastor Beyer, Jakob Pernulius from Antwerp, and a few others were with him at his death. When Flacius briefly awoke on that last morning, he prayed twice, clearly, with folded hands: "Jesus Christ, Son of God, have mercy on me."[8] He was buried on March 13, though no one knows where. None of the Frankfurt clergy gave a funeral sermon for this polarizing foreigner, so Caspar Heldelin wrote and published one to honor his friend and teacher.

Magdalena Flacius became a Frankfurt citizen in September 1575. She married Heinrich Petreus, a Flacian, on October 23, 1577. She died in 1579. Petreus, who later became a court official at Wolfenbüttel, sold most of Flacius' library and much of his personal correspondence, notes, works-in-progress, and other papers to Duke Heinrich-Julius of Braunschweig-Lüneburg.[9] Aspiring theologians and historians could do worse than digging in.

---

8 Preger, *Matthias Flacius Illyricus und seine Zeit*, 2:526.

9 For more information, see Ilić, *Theologian of Sin and Grace*, 166–84.

CONCLUSION

Life and Thought in Review

WHO WAS MATTHIAS Flacius Illyricus Albonensis? He was a man of many gifts and convictions. He was a stranger in a foreign land. He was a faithful son of the Lutheran Reformation. He was a thorn in the flesh of many of Luther's closest friends and colleagues. He had a brilliant mind. He had a challenging personality. He was a comrade and a turncoat. He was an orthodox Lutheran and a heretic. He was long remembered and quickly forgotten. Matthias Flacius is perhaps the most enigmatic of the major theologians of the sixteenth century. While I certainly hope his life and work receives much more attention, I think he will nevertheless always remain hard to nail down. Matthias Flacius Illyricus Albonensis did all things with such passion, virtuosity, and persistence in such a diversity of circumstances that there is simply too much to take in even while there is not enough to go on. Those who knew him best and longest still were befuddled by Matthias. For more than a few, he lived long enough to be both a hero and a villain.

One thing was consistent throughout Flacius' adult life: He lived under the cross. The cross defined him and his theology. The cross marked each stage of his development. He was a man willing to suffer for what he believed was right and true. In fact, for him, suffering was supporting evidence of the righteousness and truth of a cause. He found fellow cross-bearers in his study of church history, and he recorded their words and works for posterity. During his lifetime, he called and admonished brothers and sisters under the cross to remain faithful. Nothing was more important than what Christ had done on the cross, which could only be understood if one knew why Christ had done it. Christ had come to save sinners. He saved them by fulfilling the Law, suffering the punishment of their guilt, and declaring them righteous by His Word. This message of Christ and His cross cost Flacius nearly everything, but it also gave him all that he ever wanted or needed. It was the cross, confessed by Luther, delivered in Word and Sacraments, that animated, steadied, and went with Flacius from the beginning of his journey north, through his depression in Wittenberg, through the siege of Magdeburg and the turmoil at Jena, and through his nomadic existence.

Did Flacius save Lutheranism? This is a very difficult question to answer. Lutheranism was not one thing at the time. It had institutional status, even in the dark years, although there was a clear imperial agenda aimed at changing that. There were significant threats to Luther's Reformation from within and without, in doctrine and practice—almost everyone agreed on that, even if they did not agree on what were the greatest threats or who posed them. In the midst of such a contentious decade, Flacius certainly threw himself into preserving Luther's teaching with everything he had. He was a leading voice and pen in the bleakest moments after the great reformer's death. He held its theologians accountable until his death. He paved the way for the Formula of Concord, where his positions were both adopted and condemned (with a sensitivity, nonetheless, to his concerns). Just as his contemporaries debated whether he helped or hurt the survival of Lutheranism in his own day, so historians and theologians still do today.

It is hard to say that any one person saved Lutheranism. I do think Flacius would say, however, that Lutheranism saved him, even as it ground him down. In Lutheranism, he found the Gospel as nowhere else, and that is what he took hold of and never let go of, even when it must have been tempting to do so. He had no delusions about his sin. He had the same fallen human nature as any other sinner. What he said of original sin applied to him as well. He also had no doubt about God's grace. In fact, he took the position on original sin that he did because he thought downplaying the same diminished the saving work of Christ, who had saved real sinners from real death and a real hell with His astounding love and selfless sacrifice. While Flacius' assessment of the human condition after the fall into sin was devastating, could anything more marvelous be said about human beings than that God Himself took flesh, shed blood, and rose from the grave for them?

Who was Matthias Flacius Illyricus Albonensis? He was a baptized child of God. The rest is history—very interesting history, but history. Ultimately, nothing else defined him. He lived, strove, moved, and died baptized. While the cross did not mark his grave so that one can visit it today, it marked his head and his heart as one redeemed by Christ the crucified, from beginning to end and into eternity. It made him Matthias.

BIBLIOGRAPHY

Primary Sources

Amsdorf, Nikolaus von. *Ein kurtzer unterricht auff D. Georgen Maiors Antwort das er nit unschüldig sey wie er sich tragice rhümet*. Basel, 1552.

Flacius Illyricus, Matthias. *ΤΗΣ ΤΟΥ ΥΙΟΨ ΘΕΟΥ ΚΑΙΗΣ ΔΙΑΘΗΚΗΣ ΑΠΑΝΤΑ Novvm Testamentum Jesu Christi Filii Dei, Ex Versione Erasmi, Innumeris in Locis ad Graecem veritatem, genuinumque sensum emendata. Glossa Compendiara M. Matthiae Flacij Illyrici Albonensis in nouum Testamentum. Cum multiplici indice tum ipsius sacri Textus, tum etiam glossae. Quid praeterea sit in commodum Lectoris in hac editione praestitum, sequens nuncupatoria praestatio indicabit*. Basel, 1570.

______. *Altera Pars Clavis Scriptvrae, seu de Sermone Sacrarum literarum, plurimas generales Regulas continens: Avthore Matthia Flacio Albonense*. Basel: Paulus, 1567.

______. *Bericht M. Fla. Jllyrici, Von etlichen Artikeln der Christlichen Lehr, und von seinem Leben, und enlich auch von den Adiaphorischen Handlungen, wider die falschen Geticht der Adiaphoristen*. Jena: Thomas Rebart, 1559.

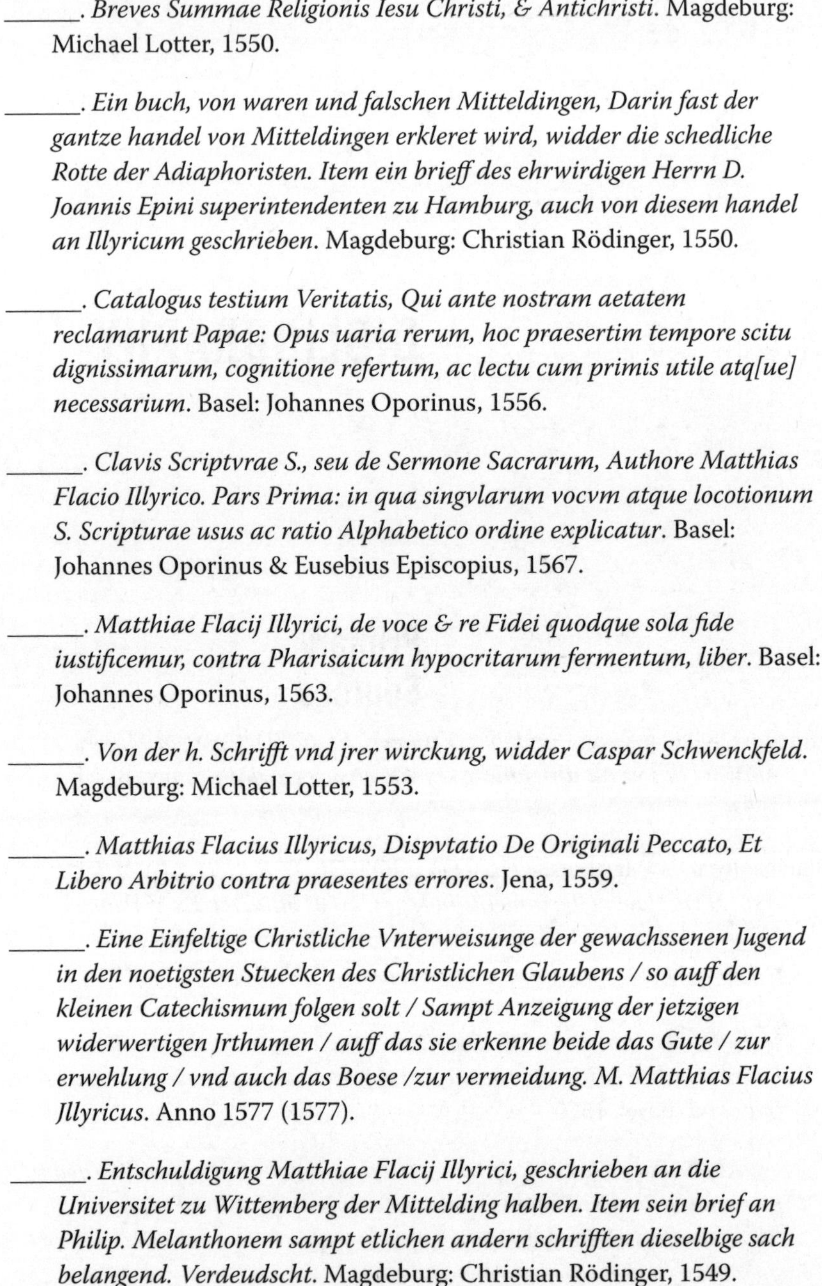

______. *Breves Summae Religionis Iesu Christi, & Antichristi*. Magdeburg: Michael Lotter, 1550.

______. *Ein buch, von waren und falschen Mitteldingen, Darin fast der gantze handel von Mitteldingen erkleret wird, widder die schedliche Rotte der Adiaphoristen. Item ein brieff des ehrwirdigen Herrn D. Joannis Epini superintendenten zu Hamburg, auch von diesem handel an Illyricum geschrieben*. Magdeburg: Christian Rödinger, 1550.

______. *Catalogus testium Veritatis, Qui ante nostram aetatem reclamarunt Papae: Opus uaria rerum, hoc praesertim tempore scitu dignissimarum, cognitione refertum, ac lectu cum primis utile atq[ue] necessarium*. Basel: Johannes Oporinus, 1556.

______. *Clavis Scriptvrae S., seu de Sermone Sacrarum, Authore Matthias Flacio Illyrico. Pars Prima: in qua singvlarum vocvm atque locotionum S. Scripturae usus ac ratio Alphabetico ordine explicatur*. Basel: Johannes Oporinus & Eusebius Episcopius, 1567.

______. *Matthiae Flacij Illyrici, de voce & re Fidei quodque sola fide iustificemur, contra Pharisaicum hypocritarum fermentum, liber*. Basel: Johannes Oporinus, 1563.

______. *Von der h. Schrifft vnd jrer wirckung, widder Caspar Schwenckfeld*. Magdeburg: Michael Lotter, 1553.

______. *Matthias Flacius Illyricus, Dispvtatio De Originali Peccato, Et Libero Arbitrio contra praesentes errores*. Jena, 1559.

______. *Eine Einfeltige Christliche Vnterweisunge der gewachssenen Jugend in den noetigsten Stuecken des Christlichen Glaubens / so auff den kleinen Catechismum folgen solt / Sampt Anzeigung der jetzigen widerwertigen Jrthumen / auff das sie erkenne beide das Gute / zur erwehlung / vnd auch das Boese /zur vermeidung. M. Matthias Flacius Jllyricus*. Anno 1577 (1577).

______. *Entschuldigung Matthiae Flacij Illyrici, geschrieben an die Universitet zu Wittemberg der Mittelding halben. Item sein brief an Philip. Melanthonem sampt etlichen andern schrifften dieselbige sach belangend. Verdeudscht*. Magdeburg: Christian Rödinger, 1549.

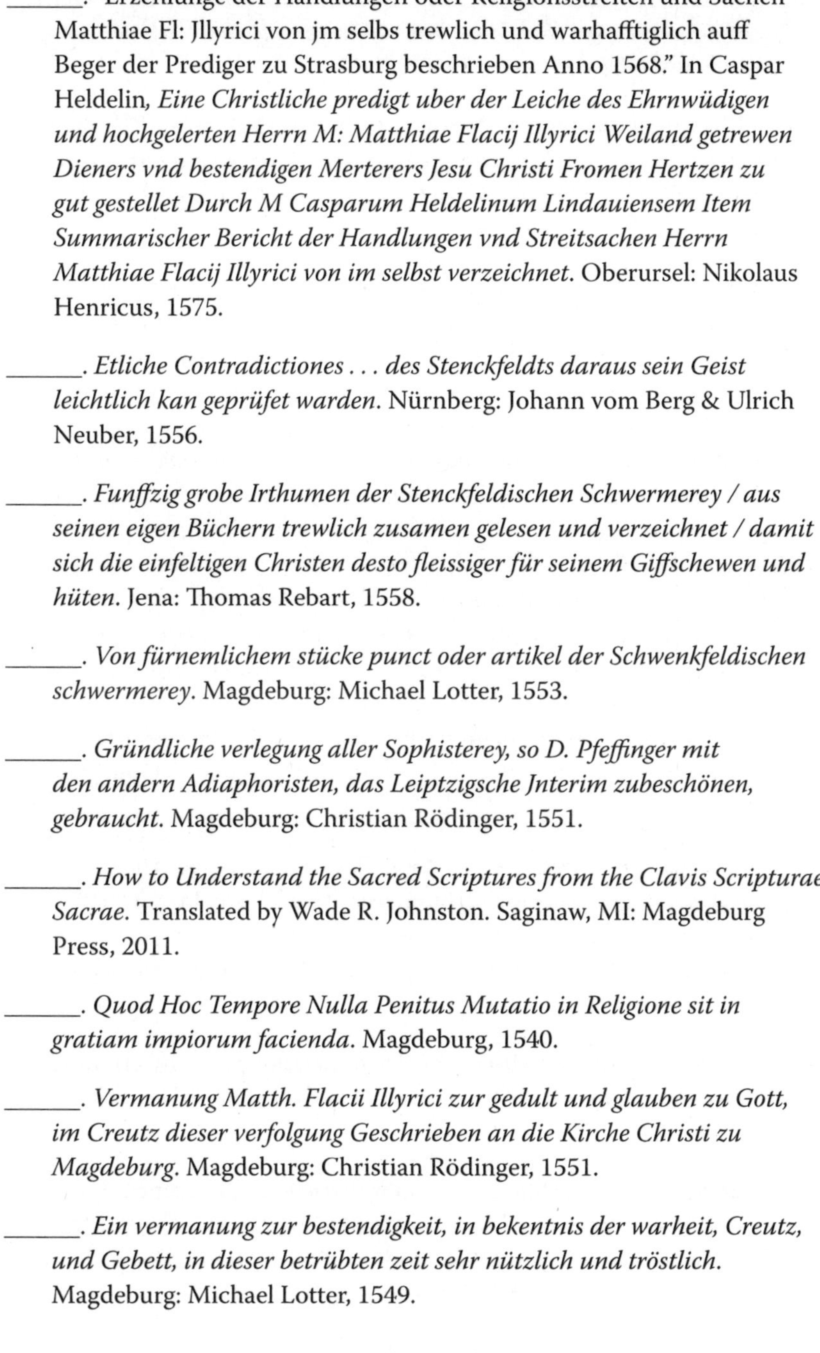

______. “Erzehlunge der Handlungen oder Religionsstreiten und Sachen Matthiae Fl: Jllyrici von jm selbs trewlich und warhafftiglich auff Beger der Prediger zu Strasburg beschrieben Anno 1568.” In Caspar Heldelin, *Eine Christliche predigt uber der Leiche des Ehrnwüdigen und hochgelerten Herrn M: Matthiae Flacij Illyrici Weiland getrewen Dieners vnd bestendigen Merterers Jesu Christi Fromen Hertzen zu gut gestellet Durch M Casparum Heldelinum Lindauiensem Item Summarischer Bericht der Handlungen vnd Streitsachen Herrn Matthiae Flacij Illyrici von im selbst verzeichnet.* Oberursel: Nikolaus Henricus, 1575.

______. *Etliche Contradictiones . . . des Stenckfeldts daraus sein Geist leichtlich kan geprüfet warden.* Nürnberg: Johann vom Berg & Ulrich Neuber, 1556.

______. *Funffzig grobe Irthumen der Stenckfeldischen Schwermerey / aus seinen eigen Büchern trewlich zusamen gelesen und verzeichnet / damit sich die einfeltigen Christen desto fleissiger für seinem Giffschewen und hüten.* Jena: Thomas Rebart, 1558.

______. *Von fürnemlichem stücke punct oder artikel der Schwenkfeldischen schwermerey.* Magdeburg: Michael Lotter, 1553.

______. *Gründliche verlegung aller Sophisterey, so D. Pfeffinger mit den andern Adiaphoristen, das Leiptzigsche Jnterim zubeschönen, gebraucht.* Magdeburg: Christian Rödinger, 1551.

______. *How to Understand the Sacred Scriptures from the Clavis Scripturae Sacrae.* Translated by Wade R. Johnston. Saginaw, MI: Magdeburg Press, 2011.

______. *Quod Hoc Tempore Nulla Penitus Mutatio in Religione sit in gratiam impiorum facienda.* Magdeburg, 1540.

______. *Vermanung Matth. Flacii Illyrici zur gedult und glauben zu Gott, im Creutz dieser verfolgung Geschrieben an die Kirche Christi zu Magdeburg.* Magdeburg: Christian Rödinger, 1551.

______. *Ein vermanung zur bestendigkeit, in bekentnis der warheit, Creutz, und Gebett, in dieser betrübten zeit sehr nützlich und tröstlich.* Magdeburg: Michael Lotter, 1549.

Flacius Illyricus, Matthias, and Nikolaus Gallus. *Provocation oder erbieten der Adiaphorischen sachen halben, auff erkentnis vnd vrteil der Kirchen.* Magdeburg: Michael Lotter, 1553.

Flacius Illyricus, Matthias, and Nikolaus Gallus. *Verlegung des Bekentnis Osiandri von der Rechtfertigung der armen sünder durch die wesentliche Gerechtigkeit der Hohen Maiestet Gottes allein*. Magdeburg: Rödinger, 1552.

Flacius Illyricus, Matthias, Victorinus Strigel, and Simon Musäus, eds. *Disputatio de originali peccato et libero arbitrio inter Matthiam Flacium Illyricum & Victorinum Strigelium publice Vinariae per integram hebdomadam, praesentibus Illustriss. Saxonie Principibus, Anno 1560 initio mensis Augusti contra papistarum & synergistarum corruptelas habita cum praefatione, in qua & Disputationis huius utilitas, & editionis causae exponuntur. Cui succedunt Rationes, cur necessaria sit cognitio doctrinae & Disputationis de Libero arbitrio: & Discrimina verae ac falsae sententia. Accesserunt eiusdem argumenti et alia quaedam diversorum scripta eiusdem Disputationis occasione, ac illustrandae veritatis gratia composita: quorum alia quidem antea quoq; edita fuere, alia vero nunc primum in lucem prodeunt: Omnia triplo, quam antea edebantur, nunc auctiora, lectuq; dignissima, & nostro praefertim seculo ad formandum rectius de praefentibus controuersiis iudicium ultissima cognitu*. Basel: Johannes Oporinus, 1563.

[Gallus, Nikolaus]. Confessio et Apologia Pastorum & reliquorum ministrorum Ecclesiae Magdeburgensis. Magdeburg: Michaelem Lottherum, 1550. Bekenntnis Unterricht und vermanung der Pfarrhern und Prediger der Christlichen Kirchen zu Magdeburgk. Magdeburg: Michel Lotther, 1550.

Synodus Avium Depingens Miserum Faciem Ecclesiae propter Certamina Quorundam, Qui de Primatu contendunt, cum oppressione recta meritorum. N.p., 1557.

Waremundus, Johannes [Matthias Flacius Illyricus]. “Eine gemeine Protestation.” Pages 143–79 in *Reaktionen auf das Augsburger Interim: Der Interimistische Streit (1548–1549)*. Edited by Irene Dingel. Göttingen: Vandenhoeck & Ruprecht, 2010.

Waremundus, Johannes [Matthias Flacius Illyricus]. *Ein gemeine protestation und Klagschrifft aller frommen Christen wieder das Jnterim und grausame verfolgung der wiedersacher des Evangelij.* Magdeburg: Michael Lotter, 1548.

Secondary Sources

Arand, Charles P., Robert Kolb, and James A. Nestingen. *The Lutheran Confessions: History and Theology of the Book of Concord.* Minneapolis: Fortress Press, 2012.

Bente, Friedrich. *Historical Introductions to the Lutheran Confessions.* 2nd edition. St. Louis: Concordia Publishing House, 2005.

Christman, Robert J. "'*Wir sindt nichts den eytel sunde*': The Impact of Flacius' Theology of Original Sin on the German Territory of Mansfield." Pages 294–315 in *Matija Vlačić Ilirik [III].* Labin: Grad Labin, 2012.

Dingel, Irene. "The Culture of Conflict in the Controversies Leading to the Formula of Concord (1548–1560)." Pages 15–64 in *Lutheran Ecclesiastical Culture, 1550–1675.* Edited by Robert Kolb. Leiden: Brill, 2008.

______. "Flacius als Schüler Luthers und Melanchthons." Pages 77–93 in *Vestigia Pietatis: Studien zur Geschichte der Frömmigkeit in Thüringen und Sachsen.* Edited by Gerhard Graf, Hans-Peter Hasse, and Ernst Koch. Leipzig: Evangelische Verlagsanstalt, 2000.

______. "Historische Einleitung." Pages 3–17 in *Der Majoristische Streit (1552–1570).* Controversia et Confessio. Theologische Kontroversen 1548–1577/1580: Kritische Auswahledition 3. Göttingen: Vandenhoeck & Ruprecht, 2014.

Fleischer, Manfred P. "Melanchthon as Praeceptor of Late-Humanist Poetry." *Sixteenth Century Journal* 20, no. 4 (Winter 1989): 559–80.

Friedeburg, Robert von. "Magdeburger Argumentationen zum Recht auf Widerstand gegen die Durchsetzung des Interims (1550–1551) und ihre Stellung in der Geschichte des Widerstandsrechts im Reich, 1523–1626." Pages 389–437 in *Das Interim 1548/50*. Edited by Luise Schorn-Schütte. Gütersloh: Gütersloher, 2005.

Gehrt, Daniel. "Matthias Flacius as Professor of Theology in Jena and His Educational Enterprise in Regensburg." Pages 35–65 in *Matthias Flacius Illyricus*. Edited by Irene Dingel, Johannes Hund, and Luka Ilić. Göttingen: Vandenhoeck & Ruprecht, 2019.

Grosshans, Hans-Peter. "Hermeneutik als Schlüssel zur Wahrheit: Die *Clavis Scripturae Sacrae* des Matthias Flacius Illyricus." Pages 175–89 in *Matthias Flacius Illyricus*. Edited by Irene Dingel, Johannes Hund, and Luka Ilić. Göttingen: Vandenhoeck & Ruprecht, 2019.

Haikola, Lauri. *Gesetz und Evangelium bei Matthias Flacius Illyricus*. Lund: Gleerup, 1952.

Hund, Johannes. "Kompromisslosigkeit, wachsende Isolation und Verfolgung: Das Exil des Flacius in Strassburg und seine letzten Jahre in Frankfurt am Main." Pages 81–100 in *Matthias Flacius Illyricus*. Edited by Irene Dingel, Johannes Hund, and Luka Ilić. Göttingen: Vandenhoeck & Ruprecht, 2019.

Ilić, Luka. *Theologian of Sin and Grace: The Process of Radicalization in the Theology of Matthias Flacius Illyricus*. Göttingen: Vandenhoeck & Ruprecht, 2014.

Kaufmann, Thomas. *Das Ende der Reformation*. Tübingen: Mohr Siebeck, 2003.

______. "Matthias Flacius Illyricus: Lutherischer Theologe und Magdeburger Publizist." Pages 177–200 in *Mitteldeutsche Lebensbilder: Menschen im Zeitalter der Reformation*. Edited by Werner Freitag. Cologne: Böhlau, 2004.

______. "'Our Lord God's Chancery' in Magdeburg and Its Fight against the Interim." *Church History* 73, no. 3 (September 2004): 566–82.

Klann, R. "Article I. Original Sin." Pages 103–21 in *A Contemporary Look at the Formula of Concord*. Edited by Wilbert Rosin and Robert Preus. St. Louis: Concordia Publishing House, 1978.

Kolb, Robert. *Bound Choice, Election, and Wittenberg Theological Method.* Grand Rapids, MI: Eerdmans, 2005.

______. *Nikolaus von Amsdorf: Champion of Martin Luther's Reformation.* St. Louis: Concordia Publishing House, 2019.

______, and James A. Nestingen, eds. *Sources and Contexts of the Book of Concord.* Minneapolis: Fortress Press, 2001.

MacCulloch, Diarmaid. *The Reformation: A History.* New York: Penguin, 2005.

______. *The Boy King: Edward VI and the Protestant Reformation.* Berkeley: University of California Press, 2002.

Mirković, Mijo. *Matija Vlačić Ilirik.* Zagreb: Jugoslavenska akademija znanosti i umietnosi, 1960.

Olson, Oliver K. *Matthias Flacius and the Survival of Luther's Reform.* Wiesbaden: Harrassowitz, 2002.

______. "Theology of Revolution: Magdeburg, 1550–1551." *The Sixteenth Century Journal* 3, no. 1 (April 1972): 56–79.

Preger, Wilhelm. *Matthias Flacius Illyricus und seine Zeit.* 2 volumes. Erlangen: T. Bläsing, 1859–61.

Preus, Christian, trans. *The Magdeburg Confession: With Historical Introduction and Annotations.* St. Louis: Concordia Publishing House, 2025.

Rein, Nathan. *The Chancery of God: Protestant Print, Polemic and Propaganda against the Empire, Magdeburg 1546–1551.* Burlington, VT: Ashgate, 2008.

Scheible, Heinz. *Die Entstehung der Magdeburger Zenturien: Ein Beitrag zur Geschichte der Method.* Schriften des Vereins für Reformationsgeschichte 183. Gütersloh: Gerd Mohn, 1966.

Whitford, David Mark. *Tyranny and Resistance: The Magdeburg Confession and the Lutheran Tradition.* St. Louis: Concordia Publishing House, 2001.